To all the women with stories to tell

SHE'S GOT THIS!

SHE'S GOT THIS!

Essays on Standing Strong and Moving On

Edited by Joanne Hartman and Mary Claire Hill

Cover and Interior design by Tabitha Lahr
Front cover photo © Shutterstock

Published 2019
Printed in the United States of America
ISBN: 978-1-7335237-0-7
E-ISBN: 978-1-7335237-1-4
Library of Congress Control Number: 2018914983

For information please visit us at ShesGotThisAnthology.com

Contents

Introduction

You may encounter many defeats, but you must not be defeated. In fact, it may be necessary to encounter the defeats, so you can know who you are, what you can rise from, how you can still come out of it.
                                                                —Maya Angelou

At the time of our call for submissions, we were optimistic about the state of affairs in our country; we were poised to have the first woman president, some of us even wore pant-suits to the polls. "Nevertheless, She Persisted" and women's marches and #MeToo hadn't happened yet. Our original working theme for this anthology was "Burnt Toast." Write about bittersweet stories of loss and letting go, we said, or funny stories of triumphs and struggles.

But then the 2016 election happened, launching a seismic shift in the inner and outer lives of women. We learned how much our experiences matter, and that, when taken cumulatively and made public, profound social change can happen.

Among our cast of writers are published authors as well as those who are just starting out, making this their first publication. They tell stories of realization and understanding, embracing the unknown, the surprising, and the unthinkable. Humor often emerges in the struggle. The essays span a range of topics: marriage, infertility, adoption, unexpected loss, overcoming fears, raising children who are transgender or have special needs, aging, relationships, identity, empty nests, and crossing bridges, both literally and metaphorically.

Individually, the women writing these pieces exemplify the tough and the strong, single notes of beauty and endurance. Together however, the notes become a symphony of determination and power, resonant with the changes we are witnessing. Our anthology was no longer about our individual lives and those transient burnt toast moments. It is more enduring. It's about who we are, our shared lives, and the attitude and support we offer each other.

A new title was needed to go with the new world order, signifying not that the battle had been won, but simply that we have the power to win it. *She's Got This* is our anthem, a confidence whispered to ourselves often enough, and now to each other as we witness women taking their truths public, as we do here with this anthology.

SURFACING

Surfacing

Dorothy O'Donnell

Two hundred or so triathletes stand on a San Diego beach; I am one of them. It's seven thirty on a Saturday morning in August. Screeching gulls wheel overhead; the sun fights to wedge its way through a crack in the thick marine layer. I shiver in my sleeveless wetsuit and jog in place, trying to warm up and loosen my tight muscles.

"Yeah, baby! Here comes another big set!" yells a buff young guy.

Hoping he's wrong, I scan the horizon with everyone else. We watch as the wave starts to form just beyond the line of white buoys that mark the quarter-mile swim course. The gentle swell gains speed as it rolls towards the sand, slowly morphing into a glassy sapphire mountain. My heart bangs against my rib cage as the wall of water stretches higher—four feet, five feet, six feet, seven—before finally crashing down in an avalanche of roiling foam. The crowd hoots and hollers. But a palpable undercurrent of nervous energy lingers in the air after the wave dissolves.

Minutes ago, the tinny voice of a race organizer warned us from a megaphone, "If this is your first open-water triathlon, or if you're not a strong swimmer, we advise you to skip the swim and just do the run and bike portions of the race."

Most of my training swims had been in my gym's indoor pool. I wouldn't call myself a seasoned triathlete. Yet I'm not a complete novice either. I've done three or four sprint triathlons since getting hooked on the sport at age forty.

I glance over at three women huddling together nearby. They wear the green swim caps that were handed out to competitors in my age group when we arrived. The din of the surf muffles their conversation, but I can tell by their furrowed brows and the way their eyes dart back and forth between the ocean and each other that they're discussing whether to bail on the swim. The knot in my stomach gets tighter when they turn around and walk up the beach to the parking lot, where our bikes and other gear are laid out. Part of me wants to chase after them. Instead, I dig my toes into the cold sand, rooting myself there through a combination of pride and stubbornness.

Today's race is my first since giving birth to Sadie, my only child, a few months ago at age forty-two. Since then, I've devoted two or three afternoons a week—hiring a sitter we really can't afford to watch Sadie or, on weekends, leaving her with my husband, Jim—to train for this swim.

Though I'm often riddled with self-doubt and anxiety—feelings I spent years trying to wash away with alcohol—I've never doubted my body's ability to handle whatever physical challenge I set my sights on. I've run dozens of races, including four marathons. I once spent two months cycling through the Pacific Northwest, pedaling up to a hundred miles a day while dodging lumber trucks on steep mountain passes and battling brutal headwinds and pouring rain.

Not long after that bike trip, I stopped drinking for good. Slowly, I put together a string of alcohol-free days. To my utter amazement, those days stretched into weeks, then years, of sobriety.

Along the way, I cobbled together a life that was even more astonishing. It was filled with ordinary things that had once seemed as unattainable to me as winning the lottery. The driver's license I'd lost after two DUIs and, at thirty, my first-ever new car to go with it. A college degree. A career in marketing and writing to replace the dead-end waitressing jobs I'd worked since I was seventeen. And my marriage to Jim, another sober alcoholic.

Together, we bought a rundown cottage near the beach, adding a white picket fence and a golden retriever puppy to turn it into a home. Almost a decade later, our lives already brimming with more than a pair of drunks had ever dared hope for, we had Sadie.

The triathlon is about to begin. I'd rather quit the race than do only the bike ride and run. But as I move behind the starting line, I'm more than a little apprehensive. A few more competitors succumb to last-minute jitters and flee the beach. As the announcer begins the countdown that will send us plunging into the water, another massive wave pounds the shore. I try to calm my breathing. I adjust my swim cap, snap on my goggles. And then the starting horn blares.

A giant wave smacks down on me. Churning water sucks me under and tosses me around. I try to kick and claw my way to the surface, but it's like slogging through wet cement. Panic fills me. I can't hold my breath much longer.

The sensation of drowning is familiar. By my mid-twenties, I was floundering in a sea of alcohol. But I was too weak—and terrified by the prospect of navigating life without it—to put up a fight.

When my alcoholic father got sober and tried to get me to go to an AA meeting with him, I refused, at first. Months later, sitting alone in my dreary apartment, the curtains drawn tight, with only my usual beer and TV for companions, it struck me with sickening clarity: this was all I had to look forward to if I didn't stop drinking.

I couldn't imagine a bleaker future. My most die-hard partying friends had traded all-night drinking sessions for careers and marriages by then—some even had babies. I wanted those things too. I set my beer on the coffee table, picked up the phone, and dialed my dad's number.

I was scared he would answer. And even more scared he wouldn't.

"It's me, Dad," I croaked, clutching the receiver like a life preserver when he finally spoke. "I think I want to go to one of those meetings with you."

⁓

As the ocean presses down on me, an image of Sadie in the butter-colored onesie I put her to bed in last night pops into my head. She'll be awake now, cooing and chirping in her crib. No matter how exhausted I am, waking to those happy sounds every morning always makes me smile. I still wonder if I'm dreaming sometimes when I hear them and realize they're coming from my baby.

My baby.

Though she arrived almost a month early and weighed less than six pounds, Sadie was born with a full head of hair and the most alert eyes I've ever seen. Eyes that latch on to me whenever I'm in their path and fill me with a sense of purpose and contentment I've never known before.

A surge of energy shoots through me. I attack the water again and burst through the surface, gasping for air. And then I adjust my goggles and start to swim.

⁓

My legs are stiff and heavy, my feet useless blocks of ice, when I stagger out of the ocean and shuffle up the beach. It feels like it takes forever to get to my bike.

Halfway through the nine-mile ride, my feet and legs finally thaw. With the swim behind me and the sun warming my back, I'm invigorated. I pedal at a brisk, steady cadence, the soft whir of spinning wheels lulling me into a trance-like state. Creeping up on a pack of riders who blew past me earlier, I pick them off, one by one.

Back in the parking lot, I lace up my running shoes and peek at my watch as I begin the 5K. *Is that really my time?* If it is, I'm on target to have my best race ever. I might even place in my age group.

As I approach the orange cone marking the turnaround point, the lead athletes zoom past me in the opposite direction, bound for the finish line. The first woman, a petite, thirty-something gazelle, cruises by. When I round the cone, I've counted only seven others. I run a little faster, easing into that sweet spot where I'm pushing myself but not overexerting to the point where I'll burn out my legs and lungs.

"Good job," I huff to a woman my age as I pass her.

The sound of her feet slapping the pavement fades as I pull ahead. I'm pretty sure there are only two or three women in their forties in front of me. It's tempting to go full throttle, but I resist the urge—I don't want to run out of gas.

Finally, I see the finish line. Adrenaline floods my belly and makes me nauseous. I pick up my pace anyway. Cheers from a clump of spectators spur me to dig deeper. Breaking into a sprint, I pass two men and a teenage girl and fly across the timing mat.

~~~~~~~~

On the drive home, I finger the clunky faux-bronze medal dangling from a blue ribbon around my neck. I can't stop smiling. I can't wait to show my prize to Jim and Sadie. I picture her eyes widening when they land on the shiny medal, her hands grasping for it.

When I pull into the driveway of our modest home with its green trim and shutters, I sit for a moment, thinking about how far I've come since the day I followed my dad into my first AA meeting. The house could use a fresh coat of paint. So could the picket fence, which sags under the weight of the now overgrown cloak of pink rose vines we planted when we first moved in. The grass is parched and needs mowing. But when Jim opens the front door and steps out on the stoop holding Sadie, I know I've hit the jackpot.

I roll down the car window and wave at them.

"Look, Bug," says Jim, pointing to my Camry. "Who's that?"

Sadie squirms and flaps her arms in my direction. I rush through the gate and take her from Jim. She dazzles me with a toothless grin and tugs at my medal. The race is over. I'm home. Safe. I clutch my grand prize to my chest and marvel, as I have every day since she was born, that she is mine and this is my life.

Dorothy O'Donnell is a writer and reporter specializing in the arts, health, travel, and lifestyle. Her articles have been featured in the *Los Angeles Times* and her personal essays have been published on *Salon*, *GreatSchools*, *Good Housekeeping*, and other online venues. She lives in Mill Valley, California, with her husband, daughter, and their singing mutt, Max.

Busting into Hollywood

Meika Rouda

H er boobs were *fine*. I had seen them bare-naked several times when I'd been her bag schlepper on shopping sprees. Linda was forty and had breastfed her daughter. What did she expect, perfect peaks? The answer was yes, she expected a lot of things.

Yet her disappearance on the first day of auditions for her film project in order to get a boob job was as conspicuous as the reason.

"Meika, you need to pick me up now!" she squawked through the phone receiver at five o'clock in the morning. Like a Stockholm syndrome victim, I rolled out of bed and did what I was told. Linda needed me. And I liked to be needed by someone that others thought had it all: the model looks, the famous boyfriend, the fabulous lifestyle. It was our secret that she really didn't have it together at all.

"I'm a writer and director with a film going into production, and I need an assistant," Linda had explained to me in my interview months earlier. It sounded creative and glamorous.

Help her with the script, move from New York to Los Angeles for pre-production, she had A-list talent attached to star in it, everything was green-lit, go, go, go.

As an unemployed film school graduate who grazed Soho art openings every weekend to drink wine and eat cheese for dinner, I jumped at the meager pay and long hours. I imagined myself on the film set helping make decisions about costumes and locations, making sure Linda had her half caff almond latte every morning, buddying up with the actors and staying out too late singing karaoke with them. A golden key to a Hollywood paycheck. If I wanted to make any money with my film degree, I needed a stint in LA. I figured I could do my time, return to New York with a producer's film credit under my belt, and earn a proper living.

On my first day as director's assistant, Linda handed me a large basket filled with vitamins. "God this is heavy!" she said, the jiggling pills pulsing like maracas. Her lips were thin and lacquered with sticky lip-gloss the color of cotton candy. "Put one pill from each bottle into a little Ziploc so I know what to take each day. It takes too long for me to open all the bottles and pour them out myself." Linda smiled at me. She was beautiful, and I understood why she always got her way. Grit and charm and a smooth Aussie accent can take you places.

The parking lot at the Century City Plastic Surgery Center was pitch black. I sat idling in my car with the heat cranking, wondering if helping my dysfunctional boss break out of the surgery clinic three days before her doctor-approved official release was some sort of crime. After forty minutes I saw a woman dressed in black stumbling around looking like a vagrant. Linda. She tripped and fell flat on her face. A small white tooth landed on the black pavement.

"Fuck," she muttered slowly, like she was spitting.

The tooth was a falsie; she'd lost the real one playing racquetball with her movie star boyfriend a year earlier. The boyfriend who gave her the caché to schmooze with real celebrities. Who introduced her to the Queen of England and forgave Linda when she quickly sold those photos to a tabloid for a quick buck. The boyfriend who helped her get this film project greenlit. Who paid her rent and bought her the designer clothes. The one who broke up with her a month ago, causing her status to decrease to regular civilian. Linda did not like being regular.

"What time is the casting call?" she shrieked. Her missing front tooth made her look like a homeless crack addict.

"Nine a.m."

"Fuck, I need a cigarette."

Linda didn't say please or thank you. Sometimes she treated me like her best friend, other times like a daughter, but mostly like a servant who was lucky to be doing her errands. And sometimes I did feel lucky for picking up her dry cleaning and taking the filters off her cigarettes so we could compost the butts. Because every now and then I went to movie screenings and had dinner with writers and actors, and I worked in an office with producers who liked me and told me I had "what it takes." Sometimes I felt like I belonged to a secret tribe of world-changers, artists, and makers. And that was the world I wanted to inhabit.

~

"Where the fuck have you been?" Kevin—our producer, the one who had secured the money for Linda's film, the one who was paying for our bungalow at the Chateau Marmont—said with the slow, calm tone of a serial killer.

"So sorry, darling." Linda couldn't smile because the dentist was unavailable that morning, so her usual, oozy charm wasn't as potent. "I had something come up."

Yeah, your bust line, I thought to myself.

The conference room table was scattered with headshots of handsome young men vying to be the costar of the film. "Who are we seeing today?" Linda paged through the headshots, deflecting, unsuccessfully, as Kevin stared at her.

"I don't need to remind you that this is a low-budget feature. We need to keep our schedule or this thing will go bye-bye." Kevin kissed his fingertips and raised them to the sky—an image I can only attribute to watching *The Godfather* too many times.

Linda glared at him, realizing maybe for the first time that life doesn't always have a safety net when you don't have a rich movie star boyfriend.

Do not screw this up, Linda. If we don't make the film, I will have nothing to show for the months I have put up with you. No finished film would mean the whole experience had been a waste of time. Like a writer with an unfinished novel, I'd have no producer credit if the film didn't get made.

———

Back at her house, I opened her mail and saw the stack of delinquent unpaid bills. "Um, Linda, you need to pay these," I said, holding up her electricity bill as the kids swam in her heated pool.

"Yes, I'll get to it." She didn't look up at me; she was glued to *People* magazine, checking in on which celebrities were single. She wasn't working on the script like she'd told Kevin; instead, she was trying to rewrite her life.

As the film teetered on the edge of implosion, Linda dated potential rich boyfriends. She was a jet careening out of control, looking for a landing strip. Her tits were perky but her self esteem deflated. She didn't care about the film project. She cared about being taken care of. When I had met her several months earlier, she'd seemed confident and creative and a renegade. There weren't many female writer-directors in Hollywood; Linda was ballsy, pushing through the glass ceiling. I viewed her as my mentor and a role model for what I wanted to be. Except it turned out she didn't really want to make her film or be a mentor for young female directors.

I stayed up late working on the script alone that night, as I had many nights. I liked screenwriting, and Linda wasn't paying any attention anyway. The next day, as the kids splashed around and Linda lounged on her chaise, her breasts rounding out her bikini top like orbs, I took a chance. "Linda," I said. "I worked on the script, trying to incorporate some of Kevin's feedback. I know you're busy and I wanted to help out. I did a lot of screenwriting in college." I smiled at her hopefully.

She looked at me over the top of her sunglasses and I almost thought a smile was forming on her lips, but instead they pursed into a scowl. "It's not your job to be the screenwriter. That's my job." She took the script from my hands and put it on the side table closest to the pool. Her son did a cannonball, and she laughed as the splash water drenched the script. "Here, you can recycle these," she said, handing me a stack of magazines with my script stuck in between.

Kevin decided to start shooting, even though the script revisions weren't completed. Then, the first day on set, while shooting our first scene, he pulled the plug. We were over budget before we had even five minutes of footage in the can.

Kevin said he could get me a job at a studio working in development, reading scripts. He encouraged me to stay in LA. But I realized I wasn't built for Hollywood. I didn't want to become Linda or work with anyone like her again. I liked experimental documentaries that maybe no one would ever see. I rarely saw a Hollywood movie, so why did I want to help make them?

Now, twenty years later, I sometimes Google Linda. Did she find the rich boyfriend? Did she make a film? The answer is no. She still looks great in photographs with her glossy lips, blonde hair, and ample bust line. But her expression is that of someone still waiting for a happy ending. Waiting for her story to begin.

My story began as soon as I left LA. I found a job in San Francisco producing TV pilots and an independent film. The contrast to Hollywood was apparent from the beginning. The filmmakers here were passionate and purposeful, mostly documentarians with stories they desperately needed to tell, stories that make our world smaller, more kind, less lonely. And after my LA detour, I found myself on the path I wanted all along: making movies that reveal the tiny truths that connect us.

Meika Rouda is a writer and producer whose essays have appeared in *The Huffington Post, Fresh Yarn, The Next Family*, and *Underwired Magazine*. She is a prior resident filmmaker for the San Francisco Jewish Film Festival and has consulted on programming for the Telluride Film Festival for over a decade. Meika lives in Marin County, California, with her family.

Vial of Hope

Carol Gavhane

A ll my life, I'd had hope. It was in my blood, a part of my being. I wholeheartedly believed in every cliché:

Don't give up.
It's meant to be.
When one door closes, another one opens.

Such candied optimism can make anyone insane. Somehow, though, I worshipped it. I believed in the power of positive thinking, that prayer would relieve me of any immediate burdens, and that if I worked hard enough, good things would happen.

My adolescence was tumultuous. Loud, angry knocks at the apartment door, landlords looking for rent money that was inevitably late. The feeling of emptiness when the spot where our car should have been parked was, in fact, empty. Repossessed. We lived quietly, four of us, in a studio designed for one, while my grandmother fished expired donuts out of the grocery store dumpster. Cockroaches scurried away when the lights turned on, and although we qualified for food stamps, we rarely used them; the shame was too great.

Growing up poor, I was determined to go to college and start anew, to create the life I wanted and needed to cultivate for myself. And things did change as I got older, partly by will, partly by chance. I am in awe that I now live in a four-bedroom Craftsman home surrounded by almost an acre of tall evergreen trees. It's not only beautiful, it offers me what I didn't have much of in the past. Peace.

Unfortunately, the peace doesn't last. In a five-year time frame, I have been pregnant six times with only one child to show for it. My yearning to have another child, a sibling for my daughter, is fading—no matter how hard I try.

The hope that has previously carried me through trying times is beginning to wane.

Here I am, thousands of miles from my suburban Seattle home. We are vacationing in paradise: thirty-nine-year-old me, my husband, mother, in-laws, and three-year-old. The warm ocean water is a rich blend of dark blue and turquoise. Small waves break gently on the shore, the sand a fluffy rug under my toes. Every inch of worry lifts from my body. There is no shock to the system as I inch farther into the sea. What would happen if I just kept moving away from shore and deeper into the soft undercurrent?

A few days before arriving in Hawaii, I checked into the fertility clinic for one final round of IVF. My husband didn't accompany me this time—he had already missed a lot of work over the last two years. Three egg retrievals. Three chemical pregnancies. Two dilation & curettages. Two rounds of chemotherapy drugs used off-label to stop cells from growing and dividing. Two ectopic pregnancies. One hospitalization. One uterine embolization. One surgery. Procedure after procedure. Heavy heartache after heartache.

If this last round of IVF doesn't work, I will move on to the next step, a gestational carrier. But if it does—can I let myself hope again? No. I can't allow myself to daydream about new maternity dresses or grainy ultrasound pictures. I am done with Hope. She and I are completely through. This most recent embryo transfer is just to placate my husband.

The sun is hot on my upper arms. I love how the saltwater washes over me, cleansing me with each wave. A baptism of sorts, a new beginning.

I did have one viable pregnancy in the mix. As luck would have it, though, the embryo implanted a millimeter away from my previous C-section scar. The odds of this happening were about one in a million, per my doctors. I don't think they had actual statistical data, but their point was like saltwater on my open wound. They were so very sorry another bad thing was happening to me, but this situation was a danger to my health, and I needed to terminate that pregnancy immediately.

"I am hoping with everything in my being for good things for you," my endocrinologist said last week. She spoke softly yet firmly. I appreciated her gentle touch.

I placed my feet into the cold stirrups, relieved this would be my final attempt with IVF. The small, sterile-smelling room had an adjoining laboratory where the actual freezing, thawing, intra-cytoplasmic sperm injecting, and sucking up of the embryos took place. In a few minutes, the photo of my fertilized egg was up on the flat-screen. The doctor called it beautiful.

With the turkey baster, she retrieved my miniscule embryo from the lab's petri dish, where he or she had lived and thrived for the last five days. I didn't pray that day, as I had in previous transfers. Nothing in the world of fertility was in my control. Prayer and hope were all I had, but that day, I intentionally left those behind.

⟍‿‿‿⟋

My first and only child shares her name with the tragic innocent in Shakespeare's Hamlet. We had reservations about this choice:

the character is too obedient, too dramatic, too sick in love. Some theorize she was killed by Hamlet's mother, while others think she didn't fight the weight of her clothes holding her down in the lake, knowing exactly what was to come. Who does this, who names their firstborn after such a morose character? We didn't really have an answer except that this fictional character's passion and loyalty were traits we held in high esteem. Ophelia her name would be.

It's raining lightly as we drive near the coast on Oahu. Earlier this morning, we embarked on a dolphin adventure. The package for the littlest kids included feeding, petting, and a photo op with a dolphin. Only fifteen minutes, only one hundred and fifty dollars. Insane pricing, but totally worth it. *Sort of like this IVF.* IVF is always on my mind, even when it's not.

The rain placates me. If it doesn't work, this last attempt, I could move on to Plan B. It's illegal to pay someone to carry your baby in the state of Washington, so I have already arranged a secret two-hour video conference with a surrogacy agency in Southern California. Having a Plan B keeps me going; it keeps me from giving in to the insistent thought of moving farther and deeper into the water.

Nuggets of Hope, my apparent drug of choice. Even though I tell myself we are through, I keep going back. A gambler who won't leave the poker table. A meth head who physically needs one last hit or he'll die. A woman who is afraid to leave her partner for fear of the unknown. I am all of these.

If I didn't know the pure joy of a child, I don't think I would have pushed so hard for another. Even if that meant jars of tears would be collected, a heart so laden with sadness I fear it would fall out of my body. My daughter is my personal hummingbird, a tiny creature with unflappable wings that won't let me forget I should continue to continue.

It's our last day in Hawaii, and we spend our morning at the beach. I play with Ophelia in the water, her little hand holding on to mine for dear life. The ocean on this side of the world never seems to be chilly—it's always warm, always inviting.

This thing inside of me, well, what if it makes it?

Ophelia tugs on my swimsuit. It's in this mundane moment that I choose to believe, one more time. Instead of looking out to sea, I look toward the shore. Instead of following Shakespeare's Ophelia, I choose to trust that, whatever the outcome, we're going to be okay.

Hope. She and I are back on.

Carol Gavhane earned a degree in journalism from the University of Southern California and now writes personal essays and creative nonfiction. This is her first piece to be published in print. She lives with her husband, daughter, and baby boy just outside of Seattle.

Misbehaving

Vicki DeArmon

My misbehaving days are largely behind me, most having
happened thirty years ago in San Francisco when alcohol
was a lubricant that accompanied me to bars and parties. There
was the classic loss of one shoe somewhere on Geary Boule-
vard, the time I flipped up my blouse to reveal my braless chest
during a bachelorette party aboard a streetcar, and there might
have been a one-night stand or two with someone who only the
morning revealed was quite inappropriate.

Now, too old for that nonsense, all my misbehaving comes
in the form of truth bombs slyly launched. For instance, when
my husband calls from the doctor to ask me why I think my
father-in-law—who is eighty-six and lives with us and suffered
a stroke last year—has such high cholesterol. The doctor wants
to know because these are rocking-high numbers, in the three
hundreds if I can believe that, my husband reports. I then con-
fess that I have been buttering his dad's toast on both sides for
months now. Because I know that's how he likes it.

Or for Valentine's Day, instead of sending out cards with
slivers of chocolate to those I love, I send a mass text with the

message: "This is what love looks like for the over-fifty-five set." Pictured in bed are my husband, with all of his elephantine sleep apnea equipment attached to his face and a band around his bald head strapping it on, and me, cuddled beside him with my nighttime eye shields covering both eyes, smiling seductively.

Sometimes the truth has to be wedged in. I might suggest to my grown daughter that she drink to excess only three nights a week, rather than the requisite five. Sometimes I record her on my iPhone as she stumbles in the door at three in the morning, after I'm awakened by the key trying to find the keyhole. (I'm not talking metaphor here; I do mean the actual keyhole.) The next afternoon, when she awakens, I try to replay the video clip for her, but she bats it away on her way to the bathroom. Some people reject the truth even when your intentions are good, but I don't think that's any reason to pull back.

Truth is a good reality check for husbands, too, who might otherwise hold onto the hope that you will age beautifully, like Sophia Loren, rather than a real woman. I give my husband regular truthful anecdotes that relieve me of oppressive expectations such as sophistication . . . like when I forgot to take my oversized headphones off before removing my sports bra only to find the ensuing tangle meant that either my ears were now destined for better support, or my breasts, each with their own earmuff sound system, could groove to Jackson Browne's *Running on Empty* and not have to wait for the sound to be routed through my brain. Making your husband laugh can counter the entire entourage of wrinkles that I never invited to this party anyway.

Sometimes I lob my truth bombs at strangers who stray out of the bounds of manners or accepted protocol. Just recently, for instance, while at the copy store, I got into a brawl with a man who insisted that the machine I was using was the only one that he could use and that I needed to dismount. I ignored him until he asked me for the third time, with a martyred sigh, how long my job was going to take. I was printing out a 330-page memoir and each page had to be specially massaged by the machine in a slow double-scan manner that was making me question whether the last twenty-five years of my life were that important anyway, so I barked, "I'm using it, GO SOMEWHERE ELSE. You're not helping anything by staring."

He retorted angrily, "I'm not trying to help you."

Clearly, I thought. *Who is?* I raised my hands and made like I was ready to wrestle and he scurried off to the far side of the store. Nothing so frightening as a woman around menopausal age guarding her copier.

And that's what I am now: a woman who is terrifying, who really might say anything. I'm like an old and still cynical Holden Caulfield, lousy with the truth. People no longer mess with me, steering clear if possible. And, honestly, I've found that to be a reward in itself.

Vicki DeArmon can't stop herself from writing painfully revealing memoir, which saves her a great deal in therapy costs. Luckily, few of her family members are readers, so it works out nicely. She also loves to read and write fiction, preferably comic. Recent publications include *West Marin Review* and *Women in the Literary Landscape: A Centennial Publication of the Women's National Book Association.*

The Test

Colleen Gonzalez

"Now, what do you think, did we just pass the test or fail it?" the driving instructor asked in a monotone voice. He may as well have been a drill sergeant yelling it in my face.

"Fail," I sighed. The road had just curved in front of me and instead of following through in my current lane I'd kept straight, entering the next lane over without signaling.

I was stopped at the red light, staring straight ahead. I did not look over at him. I didn't want to take my eyes off the road. And I didn't want to cry.

Why can't I do this? Sitting at the red light, I could feel the defeat sinking in. Everyone around me was going about their normal lives. Women scurried by with shopping bags and couples walked hand in hand down tree-lined suburban streets. No one would have imagined that the grown woman stopped at the intersection would be thirty soon and still didn't have her driver's license. Or maybe they did know: "STUDENT DRIVER" was emblazoned on the car doors. They were not, however, privy to my torture.

"Were you in the military?" I asked.

"Yes," my instructor answered. "How did you know?"

The light turned green and I shrugged. "I come from a military family." My previous instructors had been overly kind. But excuses and niceties were not going to cut it with this guy. If I hesitated or did something wrong, he asked me to explain myself.

He was actually my third instructor. After I'd failed the test twice, I called a different driving school and asked for the toughest teacher they had. His military bearing was strangely comforting, reminding me of my sergeant father. When I told the instructor I had failed two times already, his only response was, "Well, we better make sure you pass this time then, right?"

I spent my whole childhood being that one lame kid who never picked up the basic rites of passage. Tree climbing, monkey bars, and ice skating trips always left me defeated. I never imagined these traits would plague me in adulthood. Yet here I was again, the one still hanging on to the skating rink railing at the end of the afternoon while everyone else glided by.

Growing up in a big city like San Francisco, I never really saw much need for a car. It was easy to get around on public transportation. But once my husband and I decided to raise our family away from the large city, I quickly learned that driving was an important aspect of suburban motherhood. Playdates, birthday parties, picnics, field trips, and sleepovers overwhelmed our calendar, and most homes weren't easily accessible by public transportation. Still, I tried to avoid the inevitable for as long as I could. I pushed a double stroller everywhere and arranged occasional rides with other moms if an event was out of walking range. I told people that pushing that stroller on hundred-degree summer days was a great way to stay in shape. The truth was my earlier failed driving attempts had now grown into fear.

Still, I managed to get away with this until my oldest was starting school and I took a job nearby. There would be no way to get her to school, take the youngest to daycare, and be sitting at a desk by 8:30 a.m. if I didn't drive. The only problem was, now the stakes were very high. I'd be a new driver with my two most important beings in the backseat.

"I called a driving school," I said to my husband. My new job was starting in two weeks.

"Are you sure you want to do that?" he asked. He looked concerned, like he wanted to rescue me.

"Well, do we have a choice?"

He could see the fear in my eyes. "I can take them to school. I can take you to work too. Really, it's fine."

His efforts to assure me he could take care of it only solidified my stance. "No, I have to do this. You take the train every day and my job is right here in town. I've waited long enough." My voice revealed my frustration, but it was directed only at myself. "Everyone can do this. How hard can it be?"

Three instructors later, after another round of lessons with the military driving instructor whose style seemed to be working for me, I asked if I could book his time and car for my third test.

We pulled into the DMV testing lot. My instructor turned to me and, with the stoic cadence of a drill sergeant preparing his soldier for battle, said, "You got this."

I was in a haze. "Okay," I answered, staring blankly out the windshield.

When the examiner approached me, he shook my hand and introduced himself—I think. I was close to a full-on blackout. I looked back at my instructor and he gave me the thumbs-up sign.

I remembered to buckle my seatbelt and check my mirrors. I pulled out into the quiet street. Was my shaking visible? When I lifted my leg from gas to brake and back, it shook so much I was afraid it would slip. I employed a death grip on the steering wheel to keep my hands steady. I followed all of the examiner's commands and was soon pulling back into the DMV lot. I waited anxiously as he tallied up the slip on his clipboard.

"Congratulations, Ms. Gonzalez," he said. "You can take this straight to the window inside for your temporary license and picture."

For a moment I was frozen in place. My body, which had been shaking all day, now had to digest the fact that it was finally over. I had kept pushing back at my fear and ineptitude, and I'd finally won. I could be a normal mom who could get my children from point A to point B. When I held up my test to my instructor, who was standing at the back of the ever-crowded DMV, he smiled and mimed applause. I took my place in the photo line, clutching my exam paper as if it were Willy Wonka's Golden Ticket. Although there were only two people ahead of me, I shifted nervously from one foot to the other, anxious to get out of there before anyone changed their mind.

Driving will never be a skill that comes easily to me. And even though I may never spin circles in the middle of the ice rink, now I know that, with perseverance, I can learn to let go of the rail.

Colleen Gonzalez is an essayist and fiction writer living in the San Francisco East Bay. Her essays have appeared in *The West Winds Centennial Anthology* and on the KQED radio series *Perspectives.*

Barnacles

Mary Allison Tierney

The smell of coffee wafts from the airplane galley. My ears pop as the plane climbs over green hills ribboned with trails. White-frothed ribs of waves inch to shore, just now visible through the slowly dissipating, salty marine layer. Those waves have been in constant motion all the years I was not flying over. They rolled, crashed and receded, pushed and pulled, varying only in size and rhythm, while I assembled lunch boxes and managed schedules, carpools, summer camp applications, lists, and orthodontist appointments. Pressing my forehead against the cool glass of my coveted window seat, watching the city in miniature recede, I am relieved to have that Category 5 maternal hurricane behind me and grateful to be on this short flight to Southern California alone.

I discovered the value of solo travel after my two semi-adult kids reached the adorable spend-summer-vacation-not-near-your-parents stage and my teenager was signed up to be a counselor-in-training at sleepaway camp for two weeks. I accepted an invitation to share a beachside condo with a childhood friend and her family, and delighted in not being anybody's mom for a few days. The only towel I had to keep track of was mine, and sunscreen application is a snap when you only have to worry about your own. I read two entire novels, and went to museums and a baseball game. I learned that not being totally stressed could improve one's general outlook on life. Someone should do a study.

My youngest child has begun looking at colleges. She is casting out her net, spreading it wide, aspiring to haul in as much as possible. In preparation, I am sweeping the feathery down from every nook in my nest, honing and paring my world to its essential essence.

A few weeks after one of my trips, I sat on the chilly cement of our basement floor on a cushion raft surrounded by paper ephemera, sentimental memories released like a salty spray: drawings, notes, and research reports; a thoughtful haiku about candy corn; violent adolescent song lyrics scrawled in a filthy, folded spiral notebook; fine pencil illustrations of anatomically impossible naked subhumans; my daughter's brightly penned notes to her brothers—"Do NOT Eat My Food!" and "No Big Boys Allowed!" I was drowning in the damp, cold silence of the basement, no longer home to my dreadlocked gutter-punk high school boys hand-stitching band patches on their black denim vests, burning sickeningly sweet incense in a failed attempt to mask their weed-infused world, slamming the door until it splintered. The dishwasher was shushing overhead, no longer a daily ritual now with so many fewer meals.

Upstairs, the living room shelves overflowed with a stoic ceramic menagerie: a bluebird, a stack of waffles, skulls, several handprints, and an orange-eyed screaming green blob. I had dusted and adored this growing collection for over twenty years. It held one hand on my throat and one on my heart. I was choking on adorable, creative clutter.

I never intended to dump my kids' ceramic art in the garbage. I took each treasure in hand and then flipped it over to see whose creation it was. Sometimes there was a date etched in the rough, unglazed bottom, but usually just a first name or initials. All three kids had attended the same elementary school. Each had made a ceramic tooth fairy frame in kindergarten with a portrait of what the tooth fairy looked like. My younger son's frame was a gaping, snaggle-toothed mouth offering a masked tooth fairy ninja. My daughter's was blue and pink, mended with a glue gun and barely holding together. The back of the third frame, glazed a slick, fiery cadmium red, was clearly marked—with another child's name. In the twenty years it had been on my shelf, I'd never noticed it wasn't even made by my kid.

At this point, I became a Marie Kondo ninja. I emptied that shelf of joyless ceramics into a trash bag, left it in the laundry room, and expected to feel remorse. Nothing. A couple signature pieces were impossible to relinquish: a horned demon—its muscled, blue arms outstretched with three-fingered-hands reaching, its raw, scraped face a Francis Bacon smear. The second: a partially glazed, apple-green, screaming blob, rough-edged, my older son's wet fingerprints visible in the sloppy clay. It's a wonder the school psychologist didn't call.

The tooth fairy frames were the turning point. I didn't even flinch as I dumped a ten-year-old bag of valentines. As garbage bags filled, I slowly began scraping the emotional barnacles of maternal guilt off my ass.

While wading through flotsam of archived memories, an envelope surfaced with my own treasure: a Polaroid, "Christmas 1968" penned in sepia on the reverse. I'm posing in a red and white flannel Lanz nightgown in front of a toy kitchen set—play prep for setting up house, feathering the nest. Smiling shyly and holding a kid-sized broom. Santa brought me a broom.

But there is no play prep for downsizing, no tastefully landscaped Fisher-Price two-bedroom condo with a sold-separately storage unit so you can practice how to Tetris the boxed heirlooms. Barbie's Dream House doesn't include a set of her adult son's old truck tires in the garage.

Neuropsychiatrist Louann Brizendine, author of *The Female Brain*, was kind enough to tell me that there is an evolutionarily appropriate reason why my local landfill has started to overflow with my kid's creative doodles. My kid art-collecting hormone has dropped off. My estrogen has Wile E. Coyoted off a sandstone cliff. I had this verified with a blood test and put this fact solidly in the "win" column. All the usual suspects had been holding up warning signs pointing to the cliff's edge: insomnia, anxiety, night sweats, headaches, and a metabolism like molasses in January. A friend once remarked that every time she uncrossed her legs, sand came out. One doctor I consulted with casually described this as vaginal atrophy, like I'm just supposed to roll with that. Come *on*. All those years ago, dog-earing *What to Expect* books, no chapters mentioned whiskers, hairs only visible in your visor mirror in the Trader Joe's parking lot.

In keeping with my vow to reduce my stress level and unfeather my nest, my adult children's abandoned essentials have been served with a firm but loving eviction notice. I have resigned as curator of the dead amplifier graveyard, that set of not-quite-bald truck tires, and the boxes of black metal band T-shirts and CDs. This is where a fiery hot flash would serve me well, if only I could summon them at will like a superpower—harness the intense heat of my personal summer and incinerate the too-heavy-to-budge adult-boy junkyard. Then my spent ovaries and I could find a nice sunny spot in the window to nap, which is one of the choice items on my to-do list for my latest momcation.

My plane descends abruptly, threading the office and apartment buildings, and lands across the street from a busy marina, palm trees swaying in the warm SoCal breeze. The arrows on the runway point to nirvana: a few days of museums, coffee in bed, happy hour oysters by the water, and, yes, naps. During this season of transitions, physical and emotional, radical self-care is essential. Like a monsoon, taking this time for myself has the effect of coaxing dormant desert flowers of self-worth to blossom. Scheduled respites energize me to keep at the work of unfeathering the nest and encouraging my youngest as she begins to flap her wings in earnest. Her runway is freshly painted with many arrows, pointing in every direction.

Mary Allison Tierney has been writing and making art her entire life. A founding member of Write on Mamas, her writing has appeared in *The Sun, the Marin Independent Journal,* and the anthology *Mamas Write*, whose cover features her photography. She lives in Northern California and blogs at *More . . . MillVallison.*

Glass Slipper

Jilanne Hoffmann

"Wouldn't it be awesome if you and Dan got married?" Mazie said, wistful and filled with longing. She was a young single mom of a toddler, waitressing with me at an uninspired pizza place. From a table in her section, Mazie's friend Dan and his buddies raised their beers in salute.

"Hell, he's a prince," she said. "I'd marry him in a heartbeat. But he'll never ask 'cause he knows too much about me."

I laughed. I was nineteen, and single motherhood was far beyond my understanding.

Two years earlier, my freshman life in college had been an all-expenses-paid disaster of booze, sex, and skipped classes, complete with a meal plan and monthly allowance. Since then I'd lived at home, first working at Burger King and now waitressing while taking engineering classes at a local university. All expenses still paid. A car to use, even if it was the Ford Pinto Death Trap. Curfew still in place. Self-reliant? Not me.

I wished Mazie and Prince Dan had been there a few weeks earlier, the night I'd waited tables for a large birthday party. Not the balloons-and-cake kind of party, the let's-get-him-drunk-as-a-skunk kind. Twenty-five guys who worked the manufacturing line at Caterpillar Tractor Company, the construction vehicle giant. They loved turning a waitress's "Is there anything more I can get you?" into a dirty joke.

Before heading out, one of them asked if I'd smile for a picture with the birthday boy. Exasperated but wanting to be a good sport, I said okay. The cameraman counted, "One . . . two . . ." On "three" the men on either side of me each grabbed one of my legs, spreading them so the camera could get a good shot. I yelled, pulled one leg free, and kicked. They dropped me and I ran into the kitchen. I waited for them to leave, angry and embarrassed and trying not to cry. On a three-hundred-dollar tab, they left me a ten-dollar tip.

Come to think of it, maybe I *was* ready to be Cinderella, swept away by a prince.

"How do you know Dan?" I asked Mazie, stealing another peek. His permed red afro stood out six inches from his head and he sported a devil's goatee.

"Can't tell you that," she said. "But he wants your number."

It wasn't until our first date that I found out Mazie was one of Dan's informants. He was a narc. And that first date? We went to the policeman's ball.

"Jil," one of the cops' wives said. "Are you old enough to vote?"

"I'm nineteen."

A collective sigh of relief spread through the group. Nineteen was the legal minimum, and I was drinking a beer in a ballroom chockablock with cops.

Dan's friends, older cops and their wives, rolled their eyes and broke off into other conversations. I thought the eye-rolls were about me being jailbait. But they were actually directed toward the woman who had asked my age. She was a political organizer, someone they viewed as overbearing and rude since she wasn't willing to let a man talk over her. One of those feminists. To escape her questions, I pulled Dan out onto the dance floor.

Three months later, my prince the narc was driving me in his pickup truck across a bridge over the Illinois River at midnight. I pressed my back against the passenger door, my feet in his lap, and sang along with the Little River Band song "Lady" on the radio.

He stopped the truck on the bridge and said he could watch me smile forever. I gave him one long grin that sent him over the edge. "Do you want to get married?" he asked, then was silent, letting his proposal sink in. The drama! The romance!

I said yes. I was in love with the Little River Band. I was in love with the idea of being in love. I was also in love with the idea of escaping, of getting away from my parents, who patrolled my life. I was being handed a glass slipper.

Six months later, we tied the knot, but not before I caused a stir at the wedding rehearsal.

"Do you, Jil, promise to love, honor, and obey . . ." said the pastor.

I recoiled. My prince the narc wasn't expected to say those words. "No," I said. "If he doesn't say 'obey,' I'm not going to say it either."

The groomsmen laughed. My bridesmaids applauded. I turned to look at my parents, both wearing feeble, horrified smiles. I read their thoughts: *Our daughter said that to Pastor Chuck? In God's house, no less?*

At our reception, my father signed the title to the Ford Pinto over to my new husband, not to me. It felt like I was being signed over too.

When we returned from our honeymoon, my mother-in-law helped us outfit our new cottage. At one point, she watched as I fumbled with hanging shower curtain rings.

"Do rings come in bigger sizes?" I asked. "These won't fit over the rod."

She grabbed one from my hand, slammed it over the rod, then turned to me and said, "Do you think you can handle that?"

As I tried not to show her my shame, I recalled another time I had been asked that question. When I'd first started slinging pizzas, two local TV newscasters came in for dinner before the evening's broadcast. The women gave me their order for a single pizza with different toppings on each half. "Do you think you can handle that?" one said, maybe because my skirt was too short, my bubbly waitress smile too big, or because I was too blonde. I smiled even bigger and said I'd do my best.

I wanted to dress them down. Ask them if they could handle stochastic processes or explain how differential equations can describe where the tip of a robot arm is in three-dimensional space. When they left, it was clear that they couldn't handle the fifth grade math it took to leave a decent tip.

I knew I had brains, but that didn't mean I had a clue about the pragmatic details of life. Dan, on the other hand, was twenty-five. He had a degree in criminal justice and a real job. He'd taken out loans. Paid them off. I was a nineteen-year-old child. And now I had freely given away my last name to replace it with my husband's. It was expected, like breathing. But my new name never appeared on any credit card. They were all in Dan's name. And I'd also taken a different step back, quitting the pizza job and dropping out of school to live with my husband in a town forty miles away.

A month after our wedding, the caged nights began. I sealed myself in the bedroom while the guys played poker in the kitchen. I stuffed towels into the crack under the bedroom door as a barrier against cigarette smoke and lewd jokes. Before they arrived, I peed and cocooned myself under the covers of our bed to read *The Fountainhead*.

Rand's strong and strange female main character must have seeped into my subconscious. After a few short months of married "bliss," it dawned on me that my escape from my parents had landed me in a different kind of jail.

Desperate to get out of the house, I found a minimum-wage job proofreading ads for the Yellow Pages. I was the youngest in an all-woman office, but I excelled at catching errors. And I started to pay attention to other details. The proofreaders called their paychecks "pin money," like working for peanuts. Soon, I realized that this could be my future: the cul-de-sac of knowledge, of trivial worth. I wanted more.

I quit and enrolled in a full-time engineering program, earning straight A's. Dan proudly supported my efforts. After an internship at Caterpillar Tractor, programming precision metal-cutting machines and walking the line to catcalls and mechanical whistles, I accepted an internship at IBM, half a continent away, in Tucson, Arizona. I left my beaming husband home with the cat.

A couple of months later, Dan announced that the sheriff's office in Tucson was hiring. I didn't want him invading my turf, so I muttered lukewarm noises into the phone. Unfair of me, yes, because Mazie was right, he did have some princely qualities. But I had grown out of and no longer wanted his glass slipper. A few days later, he sent me flowers. I was drunk when the flowers arrived, and I wished they were from someone I loved.

I knew then that my old life was over.

After three months of tears and tense phone calls, I went back to say good-bye. Then I turned around and drove my Pinto, crammed with my belongings and the cat, westward for thirty-two hours straight. The cat cried the entire time, but I was done with tears.

In short order, I traded in the Pinto and bought a Toyota. I made friends who knew nothing of my past, and graduated first in my engineering class at the University of Arizona, beating the boys at their own game. I turned twenty-five that year, my ex-husband's age when I met him. This time, I had the apartment, the decent-paying job, and a loan. This time, I finally had a clue about life. This time, I was ready to handle anything.

Jilanne Hoffmann has an MFA in creative writing from San Francisco State University, has read at Listen to Your Mother San Francisco, and is an alumna of the Squaw Valley Community of Writers. She's also a co-producer of San Francisco's Kidquake.

Not My Story

Joanne Catz Hartman

"Hey—know what I remember about you!?" my classmate enthusiastically exclaims at our ten-year reunion, her head tilted as if a memory has taken hold of one side of her brain.

We must have had classes together, although I can't remember which ones. She was a cheerleader or songleader, not that I'm able to discern the difference, and I was an introvert—happier behind the scenes, more comfortable on the peripheries—playing flute in the pit orchestra, helping edit the school paper. Maybe that newswriting win in the county competition has come to her mind, where our school paper won best overall. That has to be it. Pictures of my friends and me filled one entire page in the local paper.

"Your mom . . ." she says, her eyes open wide in either recognition or surprise, and she slowly shakes her head.

It's not the newswriting accolade that my high school classmate remembers about me. But how does she know my mother? Did she take German lessons from Mom after I left for college?

"She told us about the Holocaust," the leggy songleader/cheerleader tells me, eyes still wide.

I grit my teeth and politely nod, not pleased. Not pleased at all.

There are some deliciously delinquent moments to remember about me in high school. The dummy we threw over the drive-in movie screen during a pivotal scene in *Chariots of the Gods*. The time I drove the getaway car in the middle of the night to empty burlap sacks of cow manure on the steps of the rival high school before the big game. If "Hey, you know what I remember about you?" could be one of these things, I'd be good with that. But it's never one of these things.

I'm The Girl With The Holocaust Mother.

Something I've been trying to escape from all my life. What I wanted most as a child was to fit in. To be like everyone else in my Northern California suburban town who seemed to have families that had been there for generations. As a first-generation American, my need to fit in was enormous.

Once, in fifth grade, I wrapped a section of my hair around a pencil and the lock took on the diameter of my yellow #2 and stayed coiled for hours. "Oh my gawd!" the sleek, straight-haired brunette who sat behind me shrieked. "How *does* your hair do that?" I did not take this as a compliment. I pulled the hood of my sweatshirt tight over my head to flatten my curls. Being otherly was my curse. Craving exact sameness was my mission. It did not always go as planned.

I wanted a mother like the others in our cul-de-sac who packed their children sandwiches of Jif peanut butter— the smooth kind—and Welch's grape jelly on squishy white Wonder Bread. Not liverwurst on challah. When Mom finally succumbed to my wishes and attempted sandwiches like the Other Mothers, it was Laura Scudder's chunky peanut butter and thick-cut English marmalade with butter on slices of dense, seeded rye. Not. Even. Close.

There were other ways I was made well aware of my family's differences. My friends' cousins and aunts and uncles lived nearby. They talked about multiple grandparents. I only had one: a grandmother. My extended family was scattered around the globe in places people couldn't pronounce or had never heard of: Czechoslovakia, Buenos Aires, Tel Aviv.

Ceiling-high, tinsel-trimmed Scotch pines and noble firs stood tall inside my friends' homes during Christmas vacation. We had a brass menorah on the fireplace mantle. Since few of my friends had ever heard of Hanukkah, my mother became the self-designated annual dreidel-teaching, menorah-lighting, Festival of Lights guest speaker at my elementary school. To say I was mortified is an understatement. I'd get fiery hot and raise my desktop to hide, wanting to crawl inside.

In junior high there were, lo and behold, four Jews, although two were siblings. In high school, a handful more. But none of them had a Holocaust mother, and mine was dauntless, eager to speak and tell her story.

~~~

At the twenty-year reunion, I'm eight months pregnant. This means frequent trips to the restroom and having to leave the warm circle of my close group of friends. It also means I'm sober all night. Without my posse to whisper "that's so and so," I'm face-to-face with someone I only slightly recognize. She's effusive and cups my cheeks, giggling.

"Oh, look at you! Congrats!" she coos. Then her smile dissipates, her giggles silenced. "Know what I remember . . . ?" her voice now a murmur.

It's not gonna be a slap-your-thighs, shake-of-the-head, can-you-believe-how-crazy-we-were reminiscence. I know what she's going to say before she says it.

I fear I'll forever be The Girl With The Holocaust Mother.

It's odd to me that the very thing my classmates remember about me is something I don't even recall. What *did* my mother tell them about the Holocaust? Was I even there?

42

Later, back at home, when I shut my eyes and try to remember, I come up blank. I have no memory of my mother speaking to my high school. Was it in a class? Several classes? In the auditorium, in front of the whole school? Like a trauma itself, I must have blocked it out, mastering the art of repression.

"When did she escape?" asks the inquisitive classmate in the bathroom.

"Uh." I hesitate. I know my mother was fourteen, and I know the year she was born, so I quickly do the math. "1939," I tell her.

"What happened to her parents?" she interrogates.

These details are at the ready—in documents, in the memoir my mother wrote, in the videos made by the Bay Area Holocaust Oral History Project and archived on the US Holocaust Memorial Museum website, hopefully for perpetuity—but I don't carry all the facts in my head.

It's a tricky question about my mother's parents' fate, and the most likely answer is that they perished en route to Belzec, an extermination camp. And while I recognize that it is simply a matter of self-protection that I never allowed myself to absorb the enormity of her losses, I still don't want my ancestral connections, or my Second Generation Holocaust label, to be the most interesting thing about me. *It didn't happen to me* is my refrain. It's not my story.

I will freely admit to taking freedom and justice and equality for granted. Feeling apart; sure, I understood that and had firsthand experience—what adolescent doesn't? But persecution? Not so much. And I certainly didn't know anyone who disliked me because I was Jewish. I didn't believe Mom when she said it could happen again.

Each time I'm recognized as The Girl With The Holocaust Mother, I tell my mother that someone remembered her story, that what she told them had an impact. She fires at me with follow-ups: *who said that, what did they do with the knowledge?*

43

I shake my head—"I don't know, I didn't ask"—not letting on that I'm disappointed that this is what *I'm* remembered for. What good would that do?

⁓

At the next reunion, more than a decade later, not everyone's hiding their gray. It's comforting to be in a crowd of so many people exactly my age. This year no one's putting positive-only spins on the stories of their lives. Spouses have been lost to cancer and divorce, children to car accidents. There is compassion and an openness I haven't seen at these get-togethers before.

When the "know what I remember about you?" happens, I harbor no naïve expectations; this time I know what's coming.

"I didn't know *anything* about the Holocaust," the classmate admits.

"Her father brought a packet of seeds when they came to get him," says my oldest friend, who's been quietly standing next to me this whole time, bearing witness.

"You remember that?" I ask incredulously. My grandfather, believing they might be resettled on a farm, took along some seeds.

Mom would love this, I think. I wish I could say I then do the right thing—that I don't put up a wall or block this classmate's revelation, that I don't think, *no, it's not my life.* Later I will be mortified at my seemingly obnoxious behavior, but for now I fall back into snarky and defensive teen mode. Muscle memory takes over and I do the long-standing routine of head nod, gritting teeth behind a phony smile, arms crossed, yearning to be remembered for anything but this.

After the party, on my own in the car, something gives way and it hits me like a punch that this time my mother won't be there when I tiptoe into my childhood home to crash in my old bedroom, now an office. I can't tell her. She'll never know.

I'm now the holder of the artifacts—the embossed Kiddush cup, the Kindertransport passport, her memoir—the memory keeper. I'm The Girl With The Holocaust Mother, whose mother is no longer here to tell her story.

I think about obligation and duty. About the many, many branches of our family tree that ended so abruptly. I think about the all-too-frequent news of hate crimes against Muslims, blacks, and members of the LGBTQ community; how my mother always cast a wide lens on prejudice, discrimination, and genocide; how if she were telling her story now, she'd bring those events to focus.

Months later I come across her presentation notes folder in the filing cabinet in my old room (between "Parents' Fate" and "Joanne's Writings") and pull it out gingerly. There they are—not the notes from her visits to my high school decades ago but more recent visits to other schools, blue felt tip pen scrawls in her scrappy half printing-half cursive on the back of old insurance forms, where I see the words my classmates might remember.

Back at home, I open the well-worn, faded folder and pull out her speaker notes for Sonoma State University's Holocaust Lecture Series. As my mother outlines her quest to find her parents' fate, this time I don't let the words slide over me. I let them in, absorbing them, seeing the story through a high schooler's eyes. It's a cathartic kind of hurt that I've been holding back from feeling, and it's time. I'm in the bedroom, and my husband is blaring the Warriors game in the living room, and my daughter is three thousand miles away on the opposite coast, a freshman in college. The dog is at my feet, but doesn't care if I weep. I don't need to explain anything to her.

At age seven and eight, people started treating me differently . . . school: rocks, spat, hit, openly humiliated, pushed off sidewalks. I read on: *Friends ignored us, became persecutors; felt rejected by all but family. My dentist: filling/no anesthetic, "I am not allowed to give to Jews."* My finger stalls at a bullet point about a classmate—the girl, a former tormenter—who helped my mother sneak out of school on her bicycle the day after Kristallnacht, the Night of Broken Glass, when Jewish businesses and storefronts were looted and smashed and synagogues burned. I let the words sink in for what feels like the first time. I perceive a favorable nod from my mother.

I remember some of these stories. These notes, once a burden, now feel like a gift.

The past stays with us. It does. And it's a part of who I am. She carried it with her, shared it everywhere she could, and now I carry it too.

Joanne Catz Hartman is a freelance writer and editor who lives in Northern California with her husband and daughter. She is a founding member of *Literary Mama* and was a columnist for *The Jewish News of Northern California*. Her writing appears in *The East Bay Monthly, Interfaith Family*, several anthologies, and other publications. Joanne has worked as a reporter and photographer for a sailing magazine, an editor at a wire service, and a writer on a New England public television show. She also spent a decade teaching middle school. Joanne recently discovered that her mother was Anne Frank's fifth cousin.

Fine

Mary Claire Hill

I pulled into the tiny lot adjacent to the soccer field and waited, closing my eyes to calm my breathing, while my ten-year-old daughter, Ruby, unbuckled her seat belt and gathered her cleats and water jug. It had taken forty-five minutes in stop-and-go traffic to get here. Our carpool had fallen through, my husband was out of the country on business, and my fourteen-year-old son, Oscar, unable to stay home alone because of his disabilities, had to come along, cutting short the two-hour afternoon nap he takes daily to keep his anxiety and behavior at bay. Abe, my oldest, would arrive home from crew practice to an empty house and no dinner.

"These are small problems," I whispered to myself. In and out I breathed.

"What're we doing now?" Oscar asked for the third time. He knew we had an hour and a half till practice ended, and the uncertainty was fueling that darn anxiety. Or perhaps it was my clipped responses and set jaw. He can always tell when I'm upset, even if he struggles to infer the cause.

"We'll go into town and get dinner, just the two of us," I said, managing to paste a smile onto my face. "And you can tell me all about the guest speaker at school today while we eat," I added, an extra enticement.

He'd been anticipating the Holocaust survivor's visit for days. "Max Garcia is coming tomorrow, Mom," he'd said multiple times. "And he's ninety-one! Isn't that amazing?"

I wasn't exactly sure why Oscar was so excited. Had his teachers, like me, impressed upon him the rare opportunity this was—to talk to someone who had actually survived Auschwitz? Was he impressed by Max's resilience and luck? I didn't know. But as soon as he got home from school that afternoon, he'd been eager to share. And I kept delaying him. I needed him to take a nap. Then I needed him to go to the bathroom, to get his shoes on, to use my phone to help me navigate the afternoon traffic to Ruby's practice.

Now, finally, sitting at a round table by the window in a Burmese restaurant with just Oscar to focus on, I was ready to listen.

Oscar, who had earlier warned that he'd already forgotten all the details, started right at the beginning. "Max's parents knew the war was bad news. So they took him to another family who hid him in their house. But his parents didn't stay—they kept working." He looked at me quizzically then, his eyes squinting. "You're probably wondering why they kept working when it was so dangerous?"

I nodded, impressed he was able to read my expression.

"Because they needed to pay the people to hide him."

My eyebrows shot up in alarm.

"I know, hard!" Oscar said. "And they could only visit for half an hour because they didn't want anyone to know he was there."

I teared up listening to him. Knowing that, of course, I'd make the same decisions as Max's parents. I imagined myself frantically trying to find some way, any way, to keep my own three kids safe. And to think that just a little while earlier I had been breathing to calm my frustration over a stupid soccer carpool snafu and commute traffic.

On and on through dinner Oscar shared the circumstances of Max's eventual capture by the Nazis, his transport to Auschwitz, how he had to share a bed with three others. He stood up and gestured to show me just how small the bed was. He talked about the scant amount of food Max was given. The death march to the next camp. And the camp after that.

Oscar sat across the table from me, recounting in vivid detail all that he could remember. I looked over at his plate—he was so engrossed that his tea leaf salad was shockingly only half-eaten, while I, the one with the supposedly normal appetite regulation, had been picking at one remaining shred of romaine lettuce for the last ten minutes. He paused occasionally to concentrate on coaxing some salad onto his fork, but then continued on, looking thoughtfully over my head when trying to recall, meeting my eyes when he wanted to emphasize. He rubbed his face and puffed his cheeks, his expressions mirroring the emotions he was feeling as he spoke, and I couldn't help but realize how lucky I was.

How lucky I was to be sitting there, with just him, with no siblings eye-rolling or trying to fill in the gaps in his stuttered speech or interrupting when he repeated a thought. No audible sighs when his face contorted with the effort of producing the right word. Just me and Oscar and a story to tell.

I wanted to do something impossible. To go back fourteen years, to the day of his diagnosis in the NICU, and show a video of this moment to my devastated younger self. I could see myself alone and shaking in a darkened hospital room, staring at the characteristics of my newborn's rare condition: insatiable appetite, cognitive impairment, short stature, morbid obesity, speech impediments, low muscle tone, violent tantrums.

"See this passionate young teen?" I'd say. "See how articulate and thoughtful he is?"

"See how smart and full of empathy?"

"See those big brown eyes and that sneaky smile? Not the fake smile he shows when you bring out the camera, but the warm one that lights up a room?"

"He is nothing you should fear," I'd tell myself.

"He's going to be okay."

"*You're* going to be okay," I'd add.

I sat across from him in the bustling restaurant, drinking in the moment and savoring every expression, every word.

After dinner, we headed back to the car, Oscar still talking about Max. How he'd survived those horrific times and had gone on to live a full life. In Oscar's mind, Max was fine now. He was okay.

Oscar buckled in next to me in the front seat. I typed the address of Ruby's practice field into my phone and handed it to him.

"Be my navigator again," I insisted, forcing a switch in topics so I could concentrate on driving. "You're getting so good at it."

He took the phone into his hands, looked down for a few seconds, then pointed the way. I saw him rub his nose and look out the window into the distance. Thinking.

"Mom," he said, his voice now soft and searching. "Am I going to be okay?"

I felt my skin prickle and my throat catch. "Yeah, you'll be okay," I managed casually, ignoring his serious tone.

"You're sure?" he probed, peering at me from the side. "I mean, I know I need help. . ." He paused for a second, then continued. "But I want to be fine."

What does he mean by fine? I wondered. Was he asking if he would be cured? Did he think his learning and behavioral challenges would go away? That, like Max, at some point the immediate struggles would end and his life would carry on, forever influenced, but not determined, by all he'd endured?

Did he want to know if he would be able to live on his own, have a job and a family? Could I tell him that I'd stopped measuring his life by the typical milestones, and that we'd figure it out, one hurdle at a time? Like I'd always done?

I knew this much: local community college classes with an aide, maybe, not dorm life in a distant city. Relationships yes,

50

but children no. Living independently, doubtful. But a meaningful job at the local zoo and friends who shared his passion for sports, definitely. Those I'd battle for.

"Are you fine now?" I asked sneaking a peek over at him. He was looking out the window again. Not meeting my gaze.

"Yeah, I'm fine now," he said, relieved.

"Then you'll always be fine," I smiled.

I had never been so sure.

Mary Claire Hill is a writer and editor who lives in Northern California with her husband and three children. She has read her essays at San Francisco's Lit Crawl and Listen to Your Mother, and her work has appeared in *Mamas Write*, on her blogs, and in other disability-related publications. She is a Lit Camp alum who is working on a memoir about learning to accept her son's disability and helping him do the same. She distracts herself by hiking the hills in her neighborhood and taking online math classes.

STANDING
STRONG

Cupcake

Kate Hopper

I am eleven years old and my parents recently divorced. My mom has moved to the top floor of a duplex on a busy street a couple miles from our house, the house where, until a few months ago, we—my two sisters and my parents and I—all lived together and where the words "separation" and "divorce" weren't spoken in relation to *our* family. I thought we were fine.

Now, our weeks are divided between the house and the apartment, our time even-steven between Mom and Dad. On Wednesdays after school, we take a different bus, one that drops us around the corner from Mom's apartment. We carry large tote bags full of clothes we'll need for the rest of the week and let ourselves into the dark stairway that leads up to her apartment. On Saturdays at noon, we head back to the house to spend the next three and a half days with Dad. Everything is new and raw, so we agree to this schedule—*Did we even have a choice?*—though the constant back and forth is unmooring. We are always forgetting things: jeans, our favorite shirts. And Mom acts too cheerful, while Dad spends too much time standing at the back door, staring out at the yard, his mouth pulled into a perpetual frown.

Mom's apartment has freshly painted white walls and dark brown industrial carpet. When it's warm and the windows are open, the apartment fills with the sound of traffic. When the man who lives downstairs has friends over, the apartment also fills with an acrid smell, like burning leaves, which I don't yet recognize.

My sisters and I share a room that overlooks the busy street. The three twin beds, each pushed against a different wall, are covered with matching homemade blue and yellow bedspreads and decorative yellow pillows on which Mom has stitched our initials. But we are not babies. We are thirteen, eleven, and ten, and these thoughtful touches do not make up for the split or for how much I miss my mom some nights back at the house, when the light from the hallway seeps into my dark bedroom and all I want is the dance of her fingernails across my back.

But I convince myself that everything will be fine. And really, it's not all bad. Some afternoons when we're at the apartment, I walk down the busy street to Rosemark Bakery. In my memory it is only me who makes this trek. My sisters remain at the apartment, or they're hanging out with friends, or they've stayed after school for some reason. I walk the six blocks by myself, sometimes with a folded copy of *Teen Beat* under my arm, which I read at stoplights.

Before I see the bakery's blue door, I can smell it—the mix of bread and sugar hanging in the air, thick as fog—and I send up a silent plea: *Please have them today.* When I open the door in a clatter of bells, I see I've been granted my wish: the display case is filled with white cupcakes topped with white bouffant buttercream. They are lined up in tidy rows like an army of brides. So orderly. So hopeful. My mouth begins to water.

A middle-aged woman wearing an apron and hairnet emerges from the back. She's always gruff and seems annoyed by my presence, though you'd think she'd know me by now, somehow understand that I need to keep coming here because my world has been turned upside down. Years later, I will understand that I had already become an expert in seeming *fine*. She would have had to study me closely to see any cracks in my veneer. And she's too busy for that, so instead she glares down at me while I fish thirty-five cents from my pocket and pass it into her rough palm.

I leave the bakery—the rumble of semis replacing the jangle of bells—before I pull the cupcake from its bag. Standing on the sidewalk in a cloud of exhaust, I gently peel paper from cake. I know I should savor it, but I can't. I take one huge bite after another, as if I'm starving. The sugar explodes in my mouth, frosting and cake, crumbly and smooth, dissolving on my tongue. And because I'm only eleven and don't understand that filling yourself up this way never works—just as I don't yet recognize that acrid smell as marijuana or realize that my sisters and I are not responsible for our dad's happiness—I down the cupcake in three bites.

If I still feel empty when I'm done, I don't acknowledge it. I wouldn't even know where to begin. Because of course, *everything is fine*. So I wipe the crumbs from my lips, crumple the paper into a waxy ball, and head back to Mom's apartment, licking the sugar from my teeth.

Kate Hopper is an editor, writing coach, and author of *Use Your Words: A Writing Guide for Mothers*, *Ready for Air: A Journey Through Premature Motherhood*, and co-author of *Silent Running*, a memoir. Her writing has appeared in a number of journals, including *Brevity*, *Los Angeles Review of Books*, *The New York Times* online, *Poets & Writers*, and *River Teeth*. She teaches online, in Ashland University's Low-residency MFA program, and at the Loft Literary Center in Minneapolis, where she lives with her family.

Boycotting the Boy Scouts

Leslie Lagerstrom

The air in the exhibition hall at the Minnesota State Fair is thick with the scent of sweaty bodies, but none of us care. It is all part of the experience our family has come to know and love. Give blood. Stop forest fires. Enroll in college. Don't drink and drive. Register to vote. On and on, aisle after aisle of information to digest, much like the mini donuts we regretfully overindulged in earlier in the day.

Heading down the last aisle, we find the Boy Scout exhibit, which is always a magnet for my husband who is a proud Eagle Scout. As I look on, my husband strikes up a conversation with the man managing the booth, and within just a few moments my intuition kicks in. Despite the stifling summer heat of August, I stand frozen with dread because I know what is coming. I know what he is going to say even before he does.

"So your dad is an Eagle Scout?" the middle-aged leader, dressed in a freshly pressed Scout uniform, asks my twelve-year-old son, Sam, while giving him a friendly pat on the back.

Ugh, I think to myself, here it comes.

"That must mean you are a Boy Scout then, too! Am I right?" he asks Sam, believing he already knows the correct answer.

And there it is, just as I predicted.

"Well, no," Sam says quietly, knowing his answer will meet with disapproval from the proud scout.

My poor child.

"WHAT?" the man exclaims with an exaggerated sigh. "But your dad is an EAGLE Scout!"

Great, now pile on the shame.

"Boys these days have too many options, right, Dad?" A sympathetic smile aimed at my husband accompanies this assumption, which could not be further from the truth. "They're just too busy and there's only so much time in the day," he surmises. "That's too bad, you would be a great scout."

Yes, he means well, but I want to scream, "Would you still think my son would be a great scout if you knew he was transgender? Would you *really* encourage him to join your ranks?"

I know the answer without asking. News reports focused on gay youth and leaders not being welcome in the Scout organization. Instinctively, my husband and I know a transgender child would fare even worse.

Instead of screaming, we offer our agreement to his assumption with a shrug of our shoulders, feeling a host of emotions all at the same time. Anger that we live in a society that does not accept people like our child. Shame for not speaking up. But most of all, we feel a deep sadness knowing how much Sam could benefit from being a member of what is supposed to be an inclusive group dedicated to preparing young boys for life.

This is the day my boycott of the Boy Scouts begins.

Since that day, I have refused to support the organization. In the fall of each year, when naive neighbors put up seemingly harmless yard signs that proclaim, "Join the Scouts," I wonder aloud (much to my children's horror) if I can remove them without being seen.

"Wanna buy some popcorn?" adorable young Cubs ask me from behind a makeshift booth in the grocery store parking lot.

"No," I say without guilt as I walk past them, glaring at their leader with disdain.

"Look! Here come the Boy Scouts!" my friends announce as we sit on the curb watching our city's Fourth of July parade.

"Who cares?" I mutter, embarrassed by my resentment.

"Do you need a car wash, lady? The money we earn will help us go to camp," a scout in his early teens inquires as I pull up to a pump at the gas station.

Looking into his innocent eyes, I barely recognize the angry voice that says, "NO," because all I can think about is how much my son would love to go to camp, but will never have the chance because they do not consider him a real boy.

As I become more comfortable talking about my transgender child, I also become more vocal about why I dislike the Boy Scouts, a statement most people find sacrilegious. *How can anyone not like the Boy Scouts?* friends and family wonder, reminding me they are as American as baseball and apple pie.

And so it goes for years. Eight years to be exact. Eight long years of harboring ill will toward an organization that publicly excludes my son yet played a pivotal role in my husband's upbringing. An organization that taught my husband how to start a fire without a match, read a compass, and be resourceful in all areas of his life. An organization that so positively influenced him that his deep respect for scouting has rubbed off on me. A nationally respected group that does not respect my child. The conflict of emotions is immense and seems unresolvable.

And then the unimaginable happens. The Boy Scouts of America reverse their stance on accepting transgender members. Standing in the kitchen, I hear the newscaster read the headline and race to the family room to catch the entire story.

"The Boy Scouts of America will begin accepting members based on their gender identity, opening the door for transgender boys to join," the newscaster reads from a teleprompter. Then a quick cut to a video of the Chief Scout Executive who shares, "We've taken the opportunity to evaluate and update our approach. I hope you'll join with me in embracing the opportunity to bring scouting to more families and children who can benefit from what our organization has to offer."

"Embracing the opportunity." I repeat these words to myself in disbelief . . . such positive words, words I never thought I would hear with regard to transgender kids and scouting. While it's too late for my child, who is now a junior in college, I find my heart full of hope, thinking not only of the boys following in my son's footsteps, who can now don a uniform with understandable pride, but also the mothers following in mine, who will never have to know the heartache of telling their son that all boys are welcome, except for them.

And with that, my boycott is over.

Leslie Lagerstrom is the creator of the blog *Transparenthood*, which chronicles her experience raising a transgender child. Her writing has appeared in *The Huffington Post*, is featured in two anthologies, and has been turned into a stage production. A lifelong resident of Minneapolis, Leslie is adjusting to living in an empty nest with her husband, Dave, whom she doesn't remember seeing the past twenty-one years.

Fat is the New Fabulous

Claire Hennessy

I was on a white sandy beach in Barbados, on honeymoon with my first husband. The sea was an impossibly clear turquoise and there wasn't a cloud in the endless blue sky. We had decided to rent jet skis and whizz up and down the gorgeous bay beside our hotel in the manner of rich and beautiful celebrities.

"Can I have the red one, please?" I asked the tanned young man with shaggy, long hair and mirror sunglasses.

"Okay, but it's not a good idea if you're pregnant," he remarked in a condescending manner, looking down at my stomach, which was protruding nicely over the first bikini I had bought in a decade.

Mortified, I just stared at him as if he had suddenly grown bright red horns and a pointy tail. A hot flush spread over my face, and tears pricked my eyes with the shame and embarrassment of having someone mistakenly think my food baby was an actual fetus.

That incident burned itself into my memory bank like a branding iron on a cow's backside. I threw away that bikini and have never attempted to wear one again. I buried the insult deep inside in my unhappy place and refused to even *discuss* the prospect of being a parent with my unsuspecting husband.

So, three years later, when I first discovered I was pregnant, I was gobsmacked. As if I hadn't just had unprotected sex for the first time in my life and then shuffled my bottom to the wall at the end of my bed directly afterwards. As if I hadn't stuck my legs vertically against the wall, thighs clamped firmly together, for thirty minutes. As if I hadn't visualized shoals of evil, grinning tadpoles racing purposefully towards my ovaries, like weapons of mass destruction about to destroy the peace and quiet of my lovely, childfree existence.

I had just been playing around, not thinking for one moment I'd get pregnant *the very first time*. It was completely *not* what some of my friends had just told me would happen. Some had been trying for years for a baby, secretly attempting IVF like some sort of baby Russian roulette, to the point where they thought the odds of getting pregnant were lower than a giant panda with erectile dysfunction. So I had rashly thrown away my contraceptives, grabbed my husband—who, thankfully, wasn't related to the panda family—and insisted he perform his marital duties, pronto.

But now that we had scored a hole in one, it wasn't only me who had mixed feelings. My husband, although as proud as a puffer fish about his manly, fertile sperm, was also a bit gutted that he would *not* now be regularly called upon for spontaneous procreative sex.

The first indication of my impending condition had come at the gym, when pounding up and down on the stepper had been impossible, as it felt like Mohammed Ali had used my tits as a punching bag. Then, a few days later, while running to get to the theater on time, I'd actually had to cradle my aching mammaries—as if I were some sort of fitness pervert, giving myself a cheap thrill as I felt myself up whilst exercising.

I bought a pregnancy test, and, when that blue line first appeared, my heart nearly stopped. I was the grand old age of thirty-one—a "geriatric mother," according to my charming doctor—and I swear I could feel my previously redundant ovaries waving flags, cheering, and shouting, *"What the fuck took you so long?"*

But the rest of me was not ready for motherhood. It was too quick. Too sudden. I hadn't had time to fully think this through. I still liked having regular showers, spontaneously leaving the house in clothes not stained with vomit, watching movies without irritating, high-pitched, squealing cartoon characters, eating uninterrupted meals *at the same time* as my husband, and using the loo alone, without a thumb-sucking audience asking me why, why, why. I had heard normal everyday activities would be curtailed with a tiny, screaming appendage clinging to my side.

Against my will, I began to notice cute baby girls toddling around at weddings, gurgling sweetly in adorable pink dresses and tiny shoes. I was going to have one of these myself, but I wasn't sure if I was cut out to be a mother. Would I be any good at it? No one I knew had any young children or babies. Both my sisters had selfishly decided to forgo the delights of childbirth, one of whom I could almost forgive because, being a Buddhist nun, she was sworn to celibacy.

The general impression I'd gleaned from TV shows and books was that babies meant sleepless nights, endless crying (including the baby), projectile vomiting, and diapers exploding with dripping excrement. Not to mention a nonexistent sex life and the complete loss of your pelvic floor. At that point, I didn't really know what my pelvic floor even was, but now I wished I'd taken much better care of it—loved it, cherished it, shored it up with load-bearing steel—so I would still be able to laugh and sneeze without it being an extreme sport.

While I was coming to terms with my feelings, I hid my slowly growing parasite from the rest of the world until a friend at work, not known for her tact, stopped me walking past her desk and exclaimed, "Have you put on weight or are you having a baby?" She looked at my T-shirt, stretched tautly over my rounded belly.

Immediately, images of that humiliating day on the beach in Barbados flashed through my mind, but instead of wanting to smack her round the face with a wet fish, I answered, "Yes, I am! I'm five months gone, actually."

"Can I touch your tummy?" she asked.

My whole body tensed. Touch my stomach? Never! No one, not even my husband, was allowed to touch my stomach! It was my Area 51. My lock-your-car-doors Bronx. My war-torn Gaza Strip. My no-go zone. Since that day on the beach, I had hidden my fleshy donut ring like it was a dirty secret, as if I had done something really bad. As if having belly fat was a sign of being a bad person, someone with no discipline or moral integrity. Like I had eaten all the pies and would be less likeable, a female Georgie Porgie.

"Sure, go ahead," I agreed, surprising myself. I pushed my baby forward as though an offering from the gods. *It's not flab*, I reassured myself, *it's my womb!*

Like a slap around the head, the benefit of pregnancy suddenly dawned on me. I was getting fatter because I was carrying a child, which was absolutely socially acceptable and not because I was a lazy, good-for-nothing lard-ass who had eaten too many chocolates and cream cakes.

As my friend placed her warm hand flat against my bulging middle, breaking a lifelong taboo, it felt unexpectedly good.

"Oh! I felt it kick!" she exclaimed.

Smiling back at her, I looked down and realized that instead of hating the ugly evidence of my overeating, I was now proud of my body for its wondrous ability to create new life. Here I was, walking around like a normal person, and yet I was carrying another little being inside me. One that wriggled and squirmed like the monster in *Alien* and yet was not evident unless you touched me.

And just like that, my whole attitude changed. From that moment on, instead of desperately trying to hide my love handles, I openly displayed my burgeoning belly, secure in the knowledge that I wasn't *fat*—I was fabulously, gloriously pregnant.

Claire Hennessy is endlessly editing her humorous memoir about how she and her first boyfriend reunited after not seeing each other for thirty years. She is hoping to finish and publish before being too old to go on a book tour. A founding member of Write on Mamas, she has been published in the anthologies *Mamas Write* and *Nothing But the Truth So Help Me God: 73 Women on Life's Transitions*. She has also performed her work at San Francisco's Litquake and Lit Crawl, as well as at Listen to Your Mother.

What's Left Behind

Lucinda Cummings

Mingus pulls me forward, his forty-pound canine body all muscle and exploding energy as he strains at the leash. His black nose grazes the earth, and he makes his snuffling sound, a sure sign that the hound in him has picked up a mesmerizing scent, and he's in full tracking mode. I wrap his leash around my wrist twice, fearing that one day he's going to launch himself into the air above the trail and be gone.

Rufus, my smaller dog, will never run away from me. He trots along just a few feet behind me, head high, as though he is proud of keeping up with Mingus's breakneck pace. We are a three-animal parade, out for our daily walk along the trail that runs through Hopkins, a charming middle-class Minneapolis suburb.

We haven't always walked here. After we adopted Mingus as a puppy and realized that he would never settle down at night unless he had serious exercise during the day, we tried the dog park, and then the no-sidewalk streets of a neighborhood full of grand houses and families I know. This wasn't right; I felt too exposed, too envious of those families with their living children and their trauma-free lives. Finally, I discovered the crushed-gravel trail that runs through the residential heart of Hopkins. I load the dogs into the back of my Forester, and we drive to the start of the trail, Mingus howling in anticipation.

The trail is just the right length for a one-hour walk, with ancient oaks and maples overhanging the path as it winds through neighborhoods of small cottages, bungalows, and ramblers. Over time, we've carved out a regular route that takes us across town, up the steep hill of a park where children rarely play, through some quiet side streets, then back on the trail to our starting point.

⸺⸺⸺

It was January 2, 2012, the day after our twenty-three-year-old son Benjamin died. Rabbi Kravitz would be coming back to our home that morning to help us plan his funeral. I got out of our bed, where my husband, my younger son, and I had clung to each other all night, unable to sleep. We were all in shock, our bodies ringing with the trauma of the day before. I knew that we had many impossible things to do that day, and somehow we would do them.

The first task was mine alone. Bob was unable to go into Benjamin's room after finding him there the day before, and it would not have been fair to ask our eighteen-year-old son Sam to do it. I waited until the two of them had gone downstairs to find coffee, then took a deep breath and walked down the hall to Benjamin's room.

As I pushed open the door, I realized I was talking out loud, praying really, "Please G-d, please help me. Please just let me be able to find this quickly." Holding my body stiff, I walked over to Benjamin's dresser. I heard myself repeating, "Please, G-d," over and over again, like a chant. I kept my eyes pointed toward the dresser, unable to face so many things in that room, and opened the top drawer.

Thank G-d, there it is. I don't have to search for it. I pulled out the bright blue-and-green batik bag, the one that Benjamin and his grandma made together just before his Bar Mitzvah, the bag that held his tallit, the prayer shawl in which my son would be buried the next day. Holding the bag tightly against my chest, I turned toward the door and hurried out, finally exhaling as I reached our room. "Thank you, G-d," I whispered.

Later that morning I said good-bye to Benjamin's tallit as I handed it to our rabbi, but I carried the empty bag around the house for days.

Walking this trail is like putting on an old shoe, broken in just right. My dogs stop to sniff and pee next to the same bushes, the same trash cans and fire hydrants, on every walk, no matter the season. They know the way: where to turn, when to stop at the crosswalk, when to turn their heads in anticipation of other dogs barking from inside the houses we pass. Rufus insists that we stop halfway through our walks in the summer to rest under the same crab apple tree, where the grass is thick and soft. Only a few times has Mingus glimpsed the beautiful cocoa Weimaraner that lives behind a certain picket fence, but he pauses in front of that house on every walk, searching for the friend he's never met.

Our walking becomes a practice, a kind of meditation. We walk as the sun grows warm on our backs and green shoots sprout next to the trail. We watch leaves unfurling above us as spring arrives again. I admire longstanding flower gardens that circle the trees on old lawns, and notice wading pools dotting backyards. When fall comes, we kick dry, crimson leaves ahead of us as the light grows sparse. We pick our way across icy patches on the trail and hurry along with the wind in our faces, trying to finish our walk before the early dark of winter.

In the beginning, my steps are labored, and I struggle to keep up with Mingus. I must build my endurance slowly, adding five minutes to our walk every week or two. When we finish, my feet hurt and my knees shake. After a few months, I notice the beginnings of strength in my calves and the muscles that support my arthritic knees. One day, I'm climbing the big hill in the park without feeling out of breath.

I hear my black running shoes crunching on the gravel; in winter, the soles of my red boots make the snow squeak as we walk along. I revel in the movement, the power to push forward, and the repetition of one step after another. My breathing grows fast and even, heels touching earth, feet rolling forward. Walking is healing; to move my body is to open up the channels where the trauma sits frozen like an ice dam. Step by step, I feel it melting, becoming fluid.

⁓

Every bereaved family has its own calculations to make when it comes to the possessions left behind by our beloveds. Not just what do we keep and what do we donate, but what will be the timeline of our readiness to face the sorting; how will we manage it, in stages or all at once, alone or together? How do we know when we are ready to part with something, or when we may feel tempted to give in to the unfortunate pressure that urges us to "let go" or "move on"?

Sometimes that pressure comes from people who think they are helping us, and sometimes from inside ourselves, where we imagine that it must be *time*, whatever that means, *time* to be emptying out drawers or bagging up clothing for Goodwill. And sometimes it's just the pressure of the unbearable pain that arises when we see a certain pair of worn Birkenstocks in a certain closet. Like suddenly ripping the Band-Aid off a wound, we stuff the shoes into a big black bag with some out-of-style clothes and set the bag on the front porch for the charity truck to take away.

⁓

One day on our walk, on a quiet street sheltered by oak trees, I spot a little house for rent. It's a square house with a pitched roof and sage green siding, maybe a thousand square feet altogether. There's a small fenced backyard, a detached garage, and white curtains at the front windows. Every time we walk past, I memorize the phone number on the "For Rent" sign and imagine myself calling the owner to inquire about when we can move in. Never mind that we own a house twice as big just a few miles away, with probably years of decluttering and repairs ahead of us before we can put it on the market. I am ready to leave today, to move into this small refuge where the dogs can play safely in the backyard and our lives will be uncomplicated by grief. Or so I imagine.

Here is the bed in which Benjamin died. His beloved Japanese tatami bed, the one he picked out when we moved into our new house, just as he started fourth grade. The bed that took three months to arrive from Japan. The futon mattress on which he slept every night, under the quilt I made for him, lying on his side with one knee propped up.

Here is Benjamin's desk, the place where he sat for hours, typing at lightning speed on his keyboard, watching two monitors at once, connecting with his world. The desk whose drawers once contained the flotsam of a passionate life: articles copied from economics journals, academic award certificates crammed in alongside concert ticket stubs, a Stride Rite shoebox full of childhood crayons, a box of condoms, computer parts he'd replaced long ago, a soldering gun, mechanical pencils by the dozens, the expired driver's license with the photo that makes me forget to breathe.

So many of the things our loved ones leave behind have voices and give off light. When they speak to us, they spin images and stories of remembered times, sometimes lit by the warmth of recollection and sometimes opening up holes at the center of our bodies where the loss and the missing still burn. These objects have a way of asserting to us their right to be here, insisting on the correctness of our holding on to them forever. Their argument goes like this: because our beloved once cherished them, there can be nothing right about getting rid of them, because there is nothing right about the absence of the one we love. It is months and months before I can even imagine getting rid of a single object from Benjamin's room.

And yet they are only things, only material objects, and there is a part of me that knows that wherever Benjamin is, in the joyous cosmology of his hero, Alan Watts, that he has let go of all of these things. They are no longer in the universe of his attention. I have his permission, somehow, to keep just what has meaning to me.

Here is the truck from the charity that gathers donated furniture to distribute to previously homeless families who are settling into new homes. The men come up the stairs, and I show them the bed and the desk that they will take away. The man in charge looks at the desk and shakes his head, telling me that it may be larger than what they can accept. My voice shakes as I assure him that yes, I read the guidelines on the charity website and I measured the desk, and it's just under the size limit. What I don't say is that he *has* to take it, that I have been preparing myself for months, moving small objects around Benjamin's room so that one day I could bear to have some of them leave. That today I am ready, and if he can't take the desk and the bed, I don't know what I will do. He has no idea what this day is costing me. But he takes the bed and the desk, leaving me with the stained futon mattress that I know he cannot take. He must sense my desperation somehow, because he offers to carry the futon down to the outside trash cart for me before he leaves.

But it doesn't fit inside the trash cart. So, as soon as the truck is gone, I drag the mattress into the back of my car, drive it down to the bottom of our driveway, and stand it up against the mailbox. The frigid November wind whips my hair across my wet face as I tape my hastily made sign to the mattress: "Free Twin Futon."

I quickly pack up the dogs and drive to the trailhead, my body all hollowed out inside. We walk the trail. And I pray with every step that the futon will be gone when we get home.

The first spring of our walking, I watch as a giant hole is excavated in an empty lot next to the trail, a towering dirt pile accumulating next to it. Cinder blocks arrive, a basement takes shape and sprouts egress window wells. Beams and rebar span the opening, followed by carpenters framing walls and securing roof trusses.

I imagine the couple who will move into this new house. They are in their early sixties, nearing retirement, children launched, and they want to downsize to a small house with all the rooms on one level. They want to be part of a neighborhood, with sidewalks and walking destinations. They like to garden, but they want a small yard with less grass to mow and lots of mature trees. When the grandchildren come to visit, the adults will sit together on the wide plank front porch and watch the kids run around the yard.

By fall, the house is finished and occupied, with wicker chairs and baskets of golden mums on the porch. Passing by, I picture Bob and me living in this little white cottage with the ocean-blue roof. Life is simple there, with my small garden and no stairs to climb, less time spent on house maintenance and more time to write or quilt. It's a fresh start, the opening of a new phase of our lives. It's a home where there is no bedroom in which our son died. Benjamin is surely with us, along with the things he cherished, but the room from which he left this world is in our past. We look forward to having grandchildren; we host gatherings of family and friends again, as we once did when our family was whole.

***

I created all kinds of criteria to guide me through the stages of sorting Benjamin's things. Was it something he'd want a friend to have? Was it something he'd be happy to donate to a person who couldn't afford a computer or an electric guitar? Was it something he cherished, or something that reminded me of happier times? Was it something that was so evocative of his sudden death that I couldn't bear to have it in my house?

Somehow I decided that nothing that belonged to Benjamin could be sold at my garage sale; I could not take money for anything that was his. But it was okay to put his battered college sofa in the "free" pile, and watch an old veteran tie it to the roof of his truck with the intention of giving it to an alcoholic friend coming out of treatment who had relapsed when his brother suddenly died. And it was okay to give Benjamin's copy of *The Riemann Hypothesis*, a book with more equations than words, to a young man who told me he was majoring in math, who seemed to love math the way Benjamin did.

In the end, the things I cherish are the things that Benjamin loved. His six-volume set of Proust's *Remembrance of Things Past*, the little Buddha he bought in Chicago's Chinatown, favorite T-shirts he wore until they were threadbare, the perpetual calendar I bought him at the Walker Art Center gift shop, the stapleless stapler that fascinated him, his copy of *Jamberry* from childhood. When I hold these objects in my hands, it is not the thing that speaks to me. It's the loving. I am holding on to my son's capacity to love, to greet life with open arms and to hold so much dear and special; his ability to love learning, and his family, and these objects that helped to open his beautiful mind. It's the loving I will keep.

Our walk comes to its end as we reach the parked car. I open the hatchback, and Mingus jumps in. He sits on the towel while I lift up Rufus and deposit him next to Mingus. I take off their leashes, and Mingus leans forward to lick my face. Grief quieted for another day, we head for home.

Lucinda Cummings is a writer and psychologist living in Minneapolis. Her writing has appeared in *mamazine*, *Grief Digest*, and other publications. She is working on a memoir about finding home.

Forty-Six Years

Carol Kirkpatrick

This morning Lily is cranky in spite of my gentle wake-up call. I'm using what I term my Sweet Baby voice, cooing her name singsong style—"Lee-lee, Lee-Lee."

"What? What is it?" she shrieks, as if a gong has shattered her sleep.

In my neutral Nice Mom voice I announce breakfast and meds, then I slide open the dark blue curtains to a blare of sunlight.

Lily sits up, rips off the headgear of her sleep apnea machine, and throws it across the bed. It's toddler behavior in a middle-aged woman. Her eye mask is skewed across her brow and her facial expression is one of disgust, as if all that sunshine were a terrible taste and she's going to spit it out.

These past forty-six years I've slowly learned that underneath the morning's rumpled veneer of rudeness breathes a tender, splendid soul whose life is a greater struggle than most. More importantly, perhaps, I remind myself, It's Not Her Fault. And like most mothers with children who have special needs, I've tortured myself with worry about how it could have happened at all and questioned whether any of it was my fault. Such a waste of time and yet so natural. I have concluded that it doesn't really matter so much how she got to be this way as how I now cope with it. The journey is bumpy and completely without road maps.

Since birth Lily has suffered from epilepsy, developmental delays, and a touch of cerebral palsy, so that her gait lags and her left foot curls under slightly. Her left leg is half the circumference of her right. Her feet are two different sizes, so we have to buy two pairs of shoes each time, which galls my Scottish sense of thrift.

Extra expenses are only a tiny part of the surprise gift package called Lily. I became self-employed when the companies I worked for weren't sympathetic about time off for all the extra medical appointments and emergencies. Her long-suffering older brother got the short end of Mom Time because Lily's needs always seemed to be raging on the front burner. That legacy continues its sibling simmer and I worry about their future together when I'm gone.

Pretty Lily and her handsome brother Joe are what the Hawaiians call hapa, in this case half Asian and half European. Lily's gorgeous dark auburn hair, brown eyes, and milky skin favor her Chinese father. With my pink skin and red-haired Celtic looks, people meeting us for the first time often assume I adopted a little Asian orphan girl. But Lily has none of it.

"This is my own mom. I grew in my mom's tummy, right Mom?" she claims me proudly, then we squeeze hands and roll our eyes.

And so, on this second morning of my weekly forty-eight-hour Mom Shift—when Lily moves to my house while her four paid caregivers enjoy the weekend off—Lily eats breakfast in the sun-blazed bedroom, squinting and complaining; swallows her seizure pills; and our day begins.

Lily moves in slow motion, her tortoise to my hare, which can drive us both nuts if we are running late. At her pace it takes almost two hours for her to get ready. After her braided hair dries, she lets it loose, doubles over and quickly flings her head back up so the rippled hair flares out behind. "Look Mom, Diana Ross!" she cries, then sings, "Stop! In the Name of Love" into her hairbrush.

As always, getting dressed is an awkward business. Once we've selected clothes that suit the weather, match, fit, and are actually clean, she needs help to straighten out shoulder seams and sleeves, which always end up in a twist due to the way she dives, arms aloft, into T-shirts and sweaters.

While we're preparing lunch, Lily insists we speak in fake Chinese accents like Martin Yan the TV chef. (Other times we imitate Martha Stewart or Julia Child.) After lunch, we drive to Costco. As we pull out of the parking lot, Lily rolls down her window and yells at my African American neighbor, "Right on, brutha!" and I cringe.

"Oh Lily, don't say that to George."

"He's my friend, Mom, he doesn't mind."

Maybe she's right, I should let go of all this politically correct stuff. *Lighten up*, I tell myself. Life with Lily forces me to, because she sees life through Lily-colored glasses, free of inhibition, which is sort of the good news and the bad news.

At Costco we line up our hands on the shopping cart handle, overlapping our inside arms so that my left arm is under her right one. This precaution was devised years ago when she lost front teeth and suffered stitches and a broken nose after falling from seizures. Today that crossed-arm insurance pays off, because just as we pass the cheese section I hear the familiar sharp snort of her sudden intake of breath, then feel the jerk as she jackknifes forward, her forehead barely missing the cart as she hits the concrete floor. My arm under hers breaks the fall this time, and although she still hits the ground, it's not with the same impact. Sometimes she takes me down too; many's the time we've depended so gratefully on the kindness of strangers to help us up or call 911. Today, though, we manage alone.

I often think people like Lily deserve some sort of award for bravery, for having the guts to keep going—whether it's shopping, to the gym, playing basketball, or just soldiering through the bittersweet struggle of each day. Their moms might qualify for a Grit Your Teeth and Do It Anyway medal.

People often think nothing of telling me what a blessing and an angel Lily is in my life. They see only the cleaned up, carefully dressed, good mood Lily—the angel. I just smile and nod in agreement, because I know they mean well. And I don't harbor the bitterness of self-pity anymore, not like in the early days of dealing with violent tantrums and power struggles and sleepless nights in hospital chairs.

I help Lily off the floor and after pausing to breathe deeply for a minute or so, she's ready to resume pushing. Later, as we load the car, she decides to give the shopping cart a good heave-ho into the corral, loses her balance, and goes down again. When I help her up this time, she's slightly pale and shaky, and her hands are clammy.

I get her to the car, my arm tucked under hers, ease her into the seat, and drive away. As we enter the freeway, she notices the aroma of Costco's famous roast chicken wafting from the back of the car. "Woo-hoo, chicken, chicken, chicken for dinner!" she whoops, as if nothing has happened. She's in the moment. I envy her capacity for that. There are thousands of books written about staying present, and she hasn't needed to read any of them.

At four o'clock (teatime in my old country), we settle on the sofa with steaming mugs and put our feet up. It's a moment to take stock and check myself for impatience, or self-pity. *Good,* I think with relief, *nary a whiff.* Now I focus back on her and notice her pallor hasn't changed. She's been more shaken by the falls than I first thought, and when she decides to make an early night of it, I'm relieved.

After I help her through the laborious nighttime routine and our favorite prayer, I tuck her in, and finally it's lights out. As I walk away, I think of how little has changed in forty-six years except my arthritis, lower energy level, a couple of ex-husbands, and her streak of gray hair and increasing seizures and falls.

Downstairs, relieved in that way all mothers feel when they close the door on a sleeping child, I plop on the sofa and scroll through inane TV comedy shows, my head-candy reward, instead of reaching for a pint of ice cream. I'm almost through another forty-eight-hour Mom Shift, and tired doesn't quite describe the confusing ache in my body and heart.

The next morning, after I drop Lily back home, I can't shake the familiar, odd relief that has me blinking away tears. The grief that surrounds the loss of all the hopes, dreams, and expectation I had for her (and our) future leaks out at weddings, baby showers, college graduations, all the so-called "normal" things we have missed. When friends pass around grandbaby pictures, I *ooh* and *aah* like a good sport, because I truly am happy for them.

But they don't have exactly what I have, which is the supreme joy of sharing such a long-lasting, extraordinarily intimate bond with a child who has become my greatest teacher. I have been forced to learn endurance, patience, tolerance, and how to be more fully present, more loving, more kind. I cannot take a single moment for granted, as things can change in a flash. All I can do is ride this glorious, mysterious wave in utter surrender, even elation, as I watch her do the same.

Carol Kirkpatrick (pen name) is a writer whose work has appeared in the *Pacific Sun* and the *Marin Independent Journal*. A retired stage actress and blogger, she is now a grief counselor who continues to care for her adult daughter who has special needs.

Not My Mother

Steven Friedman

M y son Miguel called from his dorm room. He was having trouble breathing. "What should I do?" he asked.

I told him to wait to see if the symptoms subsided. I'm a single parent, so I had no one else to consult with. When the pressure in his chest worsened a couple of hours later, he took a taxi by himself to the ER. A doctor said he had asthma and gave him an inhaler.

This isn't serious, I said to myself when he told me of the initial diagnosis. Miguel, healthy and happy, tucked with a roommate into a slightly-larger-than-a-closet room, was fine. *This isn't serious. It's not lung issues or heart problems. He. Is. Fine.*

But his symptoms persisted, so he returned to the ER the following night, only to be sent back to his cramped dorm with the suggestion that he take a Benadryl. When he called me the next day, the third straight day of symptoms, he was crying, in a state completely unlike his usual, easygoing demeanor: unable to catch his breath, chest pounding, a heaviness in his whole body.

"What should I do?" he cried. "I don't know what's wrong."

"Go back to the ER right now," I said. "Tell them how you are feeling. It's not asthma."

He couldn't stop crying, and through the phone I felt the panic and anxiety overtaking him. His roommate took him to the ER for the third night in a row.

Though I am a preternaturally calm person, I know what it feels like to have a panic attack, to shudder in fear and feel darkness envelop you. I had one once, when I was twenty-five years old, triggered by a frantic early-morning phone call from my mother, who feared my brother was lying in a ditch because he hadn't yet come home. My mother was often crippled by anxiety when I was growing up. She was so afraid I would get hurt that she only allowed me to ride my bike on dead-end streets until I was ten. And in high school, she had an outburst if I was more than five minutes late getting home.

But Miguel was laid-back. What was going on? Was he homesick? Was he having latent issues dealing with his mother's death more than six years ago? Had he been abusing drugs or alcohol? The questions barreled through my brain and I felt my generally calm demeanor eroding. I texted him. I texted his roommate. I spoke to the ER nurse who'd done his intake interview.

"Boys from eighteen to twenty-two are most susceptible for emotional crises," she said, before explaining that young men in this category have the highest suicide rates, a disturbing comment at this vulnerable moment. "I understand what you are going through . . . and how hard it is to be far away," she added.

Her words were more frightening than comforting. Miguel had admitted to me earlier that he "just wanted the darkness to go away." He'd been given an inhaler after his first ER visit and a potential assessment of anxiety after his second. Now we were dealing with something much more serious: dark thoughts and overwhelming panic.

I finally spoke to him at three o'clock in the morning. "Miguel, I can be there tomorrow evening," I said.

He was reluctant to commit. "Let's wait to see how I'm feeling," he muttered. "But that'd be nice."

I couldn't sleep once we got off the phone. My own anxiety

was mounting, just as it had flooded me years earlier when my mother hounded me in the early hours of the morning looking for my brother. I literally felt the fear spreading through me— just as it had, I now realized, for my mother on that occasion and so many others as she worried her way through parenting.

Since Miguel wasn't ready for me to come, I sent a message to my friend who lived near the college and also left a message for the university administration letting them know Miguel was in crisis and needed their help.

He took a week off from school. He tried to attend one Spanish class, his easiest of the five, but the tightness in his chest and elevated heartbeat were too much. He scrambled out into the crisp late winter air.

How could I make sure he was okay from five hundred miles away?

But then I remembered the time my mother flew out to San Francisco immediately after I'd had emergency surgery to repair a burst ulcer. She brought me the daily paper, sat with me during the doldrums of the day, watched movies with me, and befriended my roommate, Greg, who was donating a kidney to his older brother who had cancer. She was funny, friendly, and rock solid for the two weeks I was in the hospital. She was so unlike the neurotic mother of my childhood.

I called Miguel and told him I was coming that weekend.

"That would be great," he said.

I was relieved at how easy my plan was unfolding, that I would soon be there physically for my son.

I arrived Friday evening and picked Miguel up for dinner. I was happy to be there, but worried about how he was really coping and afraid to open up his emotional pain by probing more deeply the source of his crisis.

In the end, I tamped down my fears and dove in. "Miguel, time for us to lay it all out there," I said as we ate at a nearby brewery. "Do you think what happened has anything to do with Mommy's death? You rarely talk about it."

Verna died from metastatic breast cancer when Miguel was twelve. As his mother neared death, he spent nearly two weeks with a friend's family rather than be home. He had stopped reading *Old Yeller* when he found out the dog died, so I completely understood his need to be away from the death of his mother then. Maybe now that he was older, he was processing her death all over again, ready to go deeper into himself and his feelings.

"I don't think so," he said.

"Miguel, you can be honest and I won't be upset," I probed again. "Did you use anything besides marijuana and alcohol—pills or something else?"

"No," he said simply.

I desperately wanted to believe him, but a layer of jangly anxiety continued to blanket me out of worry for what might be happening to my son. Parenting alone, especially when our children are troubled, is difficult; there's no one to share your ideas—or your anxiety. My mother essentially parented on her own, too, because my father often worked up to eighty hours a week.

The next day I took Miguel to the mall to get him away from the stress. It worked. We talked about baseball's spring training, which was starting soon, and he wanted me to join a fantasy league with him. Every year I try to avoid it because I take it too seriously.

"C'mon," he prodded, "we can do it together. It'll be fun. You know you want to."

At that moment, making mundane plans to play fantasy baseball together, I felt the heaviness lift. Miguel had turned a corner. He was going to be okay. And, I realized, I had conquered that challenging aspect of my mother's personality: the anxious over-worrying. I had morphed into her good side, the person who had dropped everything to be with me during a crisis. I was here now for Miguel, supporting him through an emotional roller coaster that had scared both of us.

And I will be there the next time he needs me. And the next. Because, as I've learned, sometimes the most important thing we can do as parents is just show up.

Steven Friedman is the author of *Golden Memories of the San Francisco Bay Area*. His writing has appeared in *Rethinking Schools*, the *Marin Independent Journal*, *The Jewish News of Northern California*, and *Sports Illustrated*. Steven is a middle school social studies teacher who has a master's degree in anthropology. He lives with his family in San Rafael, California. When not writing, Steven loves reading, cycling, running, and listening to music.

Sparkles

Cindy Bailey Giauque

When my son Julien was seven years old, what he really wanted more than anything else was a sparkly blue leotard with a glittering silver star across the chest. Every week at his gymnastics class, we would enter the small shop at the front of the warehouse-like studio so that he could goggle it.

At thirty dollars it was a pricey reward for his good behavior, but he *really* wanted it, so one day I bought it.

Julien had always been attracted to shiny, sparkly things, particularly if they were pink. He loved to play in the rose-colored, spaghetti-strapped dress he had me buy him. But he also liked dressing up as a pirate and police officer, and played with cars and trucks in equal measure to dolls and Barbies. We just let him play in this gender-free zone without giving it much thought.

When he was three, he stood smiling before me one day, holding up both sides of his little pink dress, and asked, "Mom, can I wear this to school tomorrow?"

My heart skipped. One thing I love about Julien is that he is not shy; he's active, curious, and creative. I did not want to squash his self-expression. At the same time, he's sensitive, and I wanted to protect him from the scars of potential teasing.

"I would love for you to wear that dress to school. It looks beautiful on you!" I said. "But there are some kids who might make fun of you for that. So for now, let's just play dress-up at home."

"Okay," he shrugged, and ran off to play, never asking me again.

Still, his request left something gnawing in me. Had I made the right choice? Was I being more protective than supportive? I decided that when he was older, if he still wanted to wear a dress to school, fully understanding the implications, I would do everything to support him.

On the day I bought Julien the blue sparkly leotard, he was so excited that he changed into it the minute we got home and did somersaults all over our carpeted house until bedtime. Then he took it off and meticulously placed it on a hanger in his closet.

"I love it, I love it, Mommy. Thank you! Thank you!" he said, bouncing up and down with his hands clasped together.

"You're welcome! You're welcome!" I said, gathering his squiggly, skinny body in my arms for a hug.

As the next week's gymnastics class approached, he asked me if he could wear it there.

"Please say yes! Please say yes, Mommy!" he begged, standing in front of me, wearing nothing but his Ninja Turtles underwear, the muscles of his arms and chest wrapped tightly around his small frame. In one hand he held up the leotard on its hanger, and with the other he clutched my leg, his eyes pleading with mine, his expression frozen in anticipation and hope.

Flashing back to the pink dress, I crouched to his eye level. "Julien, I love this leotard! It is so beautiful on you. I'm fine if you want to wear it to class, but I want you to know that there may be some kids who think it's for girls only, and they might make fun of you."

"That's okay. I can handle it," he said quickly.

"Are you sure? I'm wondering if it might be better, for now, to just wear it at home."

"No, Mom," he said firmly. "I want to wear it to class."

I wondered if he was old enough now. Is seven old enough? My gut told me to give him the chance. "Okay," I said, nodding. "What if a kid says, 'Hey, that's for girls!'—what will you say?"

"I'll just tell them, 'No!'" He spit out that last word in a commanding shout.

"No, what?" I prompted.

"No, it's not! It's for girls *and* boys."

"That's right, girls *and* boys. You sure about this?"

His voice melted. "Yes, Mommy! Please. Pleeeeaaaase."

"Okay, then, let's do it!" I felt charged for a protest march. This, I thought, is how the true substance of a mother is made. It's all in how we handle situations like these. I imagined myself rolling up my sleeves, ready to protect my son's freedom of expression. *But*, I wondered, *can I also protect my son?*

On the day of class, Julien took the sparkly leotard down from its hanger and put it on. I had him put shorts over it, to which he agreed, and then off we went to gymnastics. Stealing glances at him in the backseat in my rearview mirror, I watched him absently strum the fingers of one hand back and forth over the silver beads of the star on his chest, his smile almost larger than his face.

At the club, I opened the door and was hit with the familiar stench of moldy socks and the loud buzz of chaotic conversation. Parents crowded behind a short wooden barrier on the left; on the right, kids balanced on beams or hung on monkey rings in various clusters of age-segregated classes.

Julien pushed ahead of me toward the back of the club, weaving through a tangle of parents and kids. He walked with his back straight, his head up, and his chest puffed out, his hand periodically fingering the beaded star. He practically beamed. I was relieved to see that no one seemed to pay him any unusual attention.

A coach called for his class and Julien lined up first. The only other boy arrived right behind him. Julien turned to greet him with an enthusiastic smile.

Immediately, the boy held up a finger and pointed it at Julien's chest. "That's for girls," he said.

Julien whipped his head in my direction, his smile gone, and waited for me to say something.

"Well, what do you say to him, Julien?"

Julien turned back to the boy. "No it's not! It's for girls *and* boys," he said firmly, holding the boy's gaze.

Without hesitation the boy shook his head and shot back, "No, it's for girls."

I wanted to slap that kid. Instead, I opened my mouth to reason with him—but it was too late. Julien's face had crumbled. He rammed his body into my stomach, locked his arms tightly around my waist, and bawled.

"It's okay," I tried to soothe him, wrapping my arms around his small shoulders. "That boy doesn't know any better. Leotards are for boys, too! They really are!" I half shouted, trying to be heard above his wails and the buzz of the gym.

By now other parents were looking at us with curiosity and concern. One mom rushed over with her phone. She was so pregnant I thought she would burst as she knelt to talk to my son. "Your mom is right! Look at this video: it's the US men's gymnastics team. They're competing in the Olympics. They're *all* wearing leotards, just like you. See that?" She held up her phone.

Bless her, I thought.

Julien twisted his snot-covered face out of my sweater just enough to catch a glimpse of the US men's team posing in white leotards and red sweat pants, then shoved his head back in the depths of my sweater, sobbing louder.

His young female coach called out to him from across the noisy room, "Julien, I love that leotard! It looks great on you! Why don't you come join us for class?"

Julien ignored her. "Let's go, Mommy," he managed between sobs. "I just want to go home."

I acquiesced, squeezing his shoulder. He had had enough. With his face stuck in my sweater and his arms still tightly grasped around my waist, I half-dragged his small body out the door and into the car.

On the ride back, he sat quietly staring out the window, his hands at his side, the smile gone. At home, he took off his leotard and hung it up on its hanger. I sat beside him on his bed for a long while, and then I wrapped my arm around him and said, "I am really proud of you. You wanted to wear that to class no matter what, and you did! You're very brave."

I knew his intention was not to be brave. He was just being himself. He had no idea he needed courage for that.

Julien didn't say anything. He just hugged me back and then got up to play with his LEGOs.

When gymnastics class came up the next week, I asked him if he wanted to go. I was thrilled that he said yes. I then asked if he wanted to wear his leotard again. Part of me wanted the battle. "I could call the coach and arrange to talk to that boy, so that he understands," I explained. "It's your choice. What do you want to do?"

He took the leotard down from the closet, laid it on the bed, and stroked the star.

"No, I think you're right, Mom," he said, his voice weighted by a thousand bricks. "It's better if I just wear this at home."

In that moment, it seemed a dark storm had moved over the colorful, open flower that is my son and ripped out half of his petals. *This is how it happens!* I suddenly realized. *This is how we grow into conforming adults!* Events like these tear out our petals, one by one, sometimes faster than we can grow them back, until one day we become people who might be afraid to try out for a team, or speak up when challenged, or follow a dream to be a painter, or even just be ourselves on the outside.

All I could do, though, was talk and model, and support and cheer my child on. It seems the substance of a mother is also made from her ability to step back and teach her children to fight their own battles. I could only give Julien the tools and inspire the courage he needed to protect himself against discrimination, to stand up for his beliefs, and to love himself exactly for who he is.

In that moment, watching him put his leotard back in his closet, that's what I promised to do for him.

"All right," I said. "Just know it's okay to change your mind, and if you do, I'll be right here to help you."

Julien soon outgrew his interest in dresses and dolls, opting instead for video games and Nerf guns. His gender explorations turned out to be more of a phase after all. Yet even now, as a pre-teen, he is not above playing Barbies with his younger sister, and he still loves the color pink, which he no longer feels the need to hide. Who drew these limiting lines across colors and clothes and activities and habits anyway? I'm thrilled when I see pink socks peeking out of Julien's basketball shoes, or when he wears his pink T-shirt to school. It reminds me that he's learning to draw his own lines through imposed limitations and stay true to himself; and if he can do that, his world is wide open.

Cindy Bailey Giauque is the author of *The Fertile Kitchen Cookbook* and her fertility story aired nationally on NBC and CBS. She's written for numerous publications, including *Glamour* and *Bay Area Parent*. An article about her two-year family trip around the world appeared in *Good Housekeeping*.

Bulldog

Christina Julian

My fantasy of giving birth to a mini-me—equipped with my signature ski slope nose and penchant for frosting over cake and sports over stilettos—died in a sterile doctor's office. He talked about premature ovarian failure and finished with our sole option for having a child: egg donation.

Hire some young filly to do the job that I as a woman was born to do?

Never.

Days later, I'm snarfing down a cherry dip cone at Dairy Queen. As the ice cream glides down my chute, it instantly transports me back to summer days spent racing through the neighborhood to DQ on my bike like only a tween could do—but clacking kids and their fertile parents break me out of my reverie and remind me that my sprightly young self is gone, right along with my ability to procreate like a real woman.

I lick away my anger and feelings of inadequacy, wishing it would help. By the time I finish, the toddlers and tweens and their do-gooding parents have dispersed, leaving me with only one thought: eating a kiddy cone, alone, sucks. It sucks so bad that I decide to stop sulking about my barren bod and get down to business. I live in a time where science affords us the opportunity to do what our bodies can't. All that's left is to hijack someone else's eggs as my own.

I'm not sure if it's the sugar high or the realization that the only one standing in the way of us starting a family is me. Either way, the egg donor hunt is on.

By the time I get home, brief my husband, and take to the internet, I'm back to feeling sorry for myself. It's hard to know if it's because I've spent two hours bundled in a pathetic, sleeved Smurf blanket scouring the internet for egg donors or because my sugar buzz has bombed big time, but regardless, I feel defeated.

None of this seems to have any effect on my husband, who not-so-silently snoozes beside me. I imagine what it would be like to sniff that sweet scent of newborn baby. And then my mind wanders back to that dream of shared DQ cones and blizzards slurped through a single straw—a mini-me at my side.

Technology is awesome, but this particular search blows. In all the romanticized versions of my life none of them include trolling the web for egg donors. I can hear my mother now: "You're doing what? And it's costing how much? And you won't even be genetically related to your own baby?"

The last time I waged such an assault over the internet airwaves was a decade ago, when I turned the web upside down in search of a man to "complete" me. If I thought the pressure was on then, it had nothing on hunting and pecking in search of the younger, prettier, viable-egg-version of myself.

I'll go along with this, I tell myself, *on one condition: This girl must look like me.* Brown hair, brown eyes, and short in stature for starters. The last thing I want is some glamazon as my fertility counterpart, reminding me that I've fallen short not only in the baby-making department but also in length.

It's amazing what you can stipulate in these searches, from GPA and hair color to ethnicity and genetic history.

The first contender wears a tight skirt, yellow tube top, and patent leather spiked heels. She clearly doesn't realize this is not OkCupid, for Christ's sake. It's egg donation. Purity and not sex should sell in this instance. I ponder if this tart of today will produce a good egg of tomorrow. It doesn't matter; she looks nothing like me.

Two hours of searching, and no one measures up. I tap my husband, who pops up, startled.

"What's wrong?"

I'm web surfing for egg donors while swathed in a kiddie blanket that my not-so-well-intended sister-in-law gave me for a present. The better question is, *What's right?*

"No one resembles me," I say as I thrust the keyboard into his lap.

"Maybe you should get some sleep and try again in the morning," he says.

My look tells him otherwise.

"Maybe your search is too limiting. Don't we just want someone who is young, smart, and has a solid genetic history?"

Because he's not hormonal, and barren, and crazy like me in this moment, I consider his comment. My mind races back to my dizzying days of online dating, when "relaxing" my standards landed me on countless reality TV–worthy dates, one of which included a night out with a closeted snake tamer.

I change eye and hair to all colors and try to dismiss my lifelong notion that blonde-haired, blue-eyed types lack depth. Then I open up ethnicity.

The new search yields more than fifty candidates. The first one looks anorexic. The next has eyes as beady as my loyal rat terrier's. I sift through just-barely-heartfelt prose from coeds detailing why they want to save our infertile souls. The ones that wax on about helping a couple in need brand themselves immediately untrustworthy. It's hard to believe the thousands of dollars in donor compensation has nothing to do with their decision to donate.

As I flip through each profile, I nix almost every one. This person must have at least one characteristic I can call my own. The schnoz will have to be it.

By the time the sun rises, I've narrowed the list to a blonde and a brunette, both with renditions of my ski slope nose, smallish in size and slightly turned up at the tip. At last I can sleep.

I wake to my husband pattering around in the bedroom. He might even be whistling, which is irksome. As is the fact that he appears to be well-rested and oblivious to my torment.

"After searching all night, I found two," I say, willing him to stop tweeting like a songbird amped up on Red Bull.

"I'm late for work," he says. "Do we have to do this now?"

My look indicates we do.

He scoots in next to me. "Show me what you found."

I pull up the donors and try to read his reaction. "They're both first-timers with excellent fertility stats," I say. "And they're under twenty-five, which should ensure success, according to my research."

He reviews the profiles with the same attention to detail as when he picks a show to binge-watch on Netflix. That is, none. "They look good to me, you decide. I'm happy if you're happy."

Happy is the furthest thing from what I'm feeling.

He zips off to work; I return to my laptop to overthink *our* supposed decision.

After one too many minutes of looking at the donor database all over again, I shift gears to work on that wine review I should have turned into my editor hours ago. Writing about booze feels mildly comforting, since all I feel like doing right now is drinking. But alcohol is taboo once you hop aboard the fertility treatment choo-choo train. I bounce about all over the donor site again to reassure myself that we (as in me) are making the right call for an egg mama.

When I can take the stress cycle no more, I email the clinic. The brunette it is. The power of a similar shade of hair cannot be underestimated in these circumstances. Or so I try to tell myself. Over and over again, all day long, while I wait for a response.

The sunset looms. Out of desperation, I go for a run, in hopes that while I'm gone an email will materialize, just like when you leave the table at a restaurant to pee and find a meal waiting when you return.

Sweating out the stress does me good, as does seeing my husband at home and on my laptop when I return. "We heard from the clinic; the donor is a go," he says, looking like he might break into song. He flips up his thumb and threatens to high-five me.

I try to hold my happiness inside, but fail. Dance party ensues.

Despite all the high jinx and jigs we dance, we ultimately face an abort mission with Miss Brown Locks. Despite her cute nose and striking hair, her eggs turn out to be duds too.

Right as I am about to break into a rendition of the boohoo blues, I remember some parting words from my very first boss, the guy who groomed me to dominate the dot-com workforce back when I was a young, overworked, and underpaid marketing tech geek and loving every second of it. "You are a bulldog when you wanna be," he said. "You never give up, which can work for or against you. What's it gonna be?"

I decide to put my supposed super powers to good use. My eggs may be fried, but my inner bulldog refuses to die. I jump back on the fertility horse and stay there for days until I unearth the thoroughbred of egg donors. The fact that she stands five foot eleven and has striking Icelandic features—basically the diametric opposite of my squat Anglo self—no longer matters. Her track record, in the form of three successful egg donation rounds, does.

Months later, I'm reminded of another mantra my boss used to like to chant, right after he slugged me in the forearm: "Being a bulldog pays!" And sure enough, it does. I land not one but *two* babies.

Fast-forward three years. Mother's Day arrives. A holiday that I am now rightfully able to celebrate. And despite all the fatigue and sleep deprivation that comes with twins, I celebrate the hell out of this day. Frets over failed femalehood and dead eggs were obliterated the moment Cindy and Dakota, in all their towheaded and sparkly blue/green-eyed glory, shot onto the scene.

They may not have inherited my ski slope nose or my chestnut-brown hair, but there is absolutely no question about who they take after in the bulldog department. Especially when it comes to fighting for what they want—more candy and toys, cuddle sandwiches, and most of all, hugs. Biology is one thing, but the baby/mama connection is nothing short of boundless. Regardless of how they got here, there is no denying it: they're my babies, from the top of their flaxen-haired heads straight through to their hearts, which beat with abandon, right next to mine.

Christina Julian is the author of the romantic comedy *The Dating Bender*, a 2017 American Book Fest Best Book Awards finalist. A wine and food columnist living in Napa Valley, her work has appeared in the *Wine Enthusiast*, the *San Francisco Chronicle*, and *Weddings California*.

The Oak Tree

Mindy Uhrlaub

Kirk was a six-foot-tall cowboy with crow's feet when I met him on the corner of Sunset and Vine in 1999. We were both filmmakers, and it didn't take long for me to fall for him. On our wedding day, all eighty of our guests joined us in the shade of a majestic valley oak in the Wine Country. That night, we gazed at the stars from beneath its branches and felt that we were home.

Five years later, eleven months after our first son Ethan was born, Kirk started feeling unwell. As Ethan took his first wobbly steps, Kirk underwent a month of radiation treatments for lymphoma. His prognosis was fair, and the oncologist reassured us that with monitoring twice a year, Kirk would be safe. He went to work at a high-end adventure travel company. He hiked and biked and traveled. He played on the floor with Ethan. We conceived our second son, Alex. Still, I worried.

Six years later, after house hunting for months, we stumbled on the perfect place. The house was a fixer-upper, at best. But we fell in love with the oak tree that stood majestically in the rear corner of the yard. The limbs of the oak were so long that they spanned over three other properties. If the four of us stood in a circle and held hands, we barely made it around the trunk.

We bought the land, knocked down the moldy hovel, and built a new house. The entire backside of our new home was glass so we could gaze upon the eighty-foot-tall tree. We watched our sons and their friends play on the tire swing that hung from a massive limb. On sunny days, our dog lazed for hours on his back under the oak tree. We tracked the arrival of screech owls, robins, and mourning doves that used it as a temporary nesting place each year.

Four years after we settled into our new home, Kirk went in for an MRI of a painful shoulder. It showed a torn rotator cuff and several tumors in the scapula, humerus, and clavicle. It was November, and the holidays were upon us. We tried to carry on, but it was impossible. Kirk whimpered in his sleep when he rolled onto his bad shoulder. He was testy during the day, snapping at the kids for the smallest infraction. Each morning, I woke up bleary-eyed, got the kids off to school, ate breakfast, and got right back in bed to cry for fifteen minutes. Then I dressed and started my day.

By December, a PET scan had confirmed the presence of cancer not only in Kirk's humerus, scapula, and clavicle, but also his acromion, testicles, aortic lymph nodes, ribs, and femur. In order to determine the type of cancer, Kirk endured a painful and invasive needle biopsy of the humerus. The test came back inconclusive. His oncologist ordered another excruciating biopsy of the scapula. Also inconclusive. Then came the needle biopsy of the femur. Once again, inconclusive. Without knowing the exact type of cancer, there was no treatment.

The next fall, after California's longest drought, came unrelenting rains. The flood siren in our town sounded regularly, announcing that the creek had overflowed its banks. Sixty-mile-per-hour winds ripped off roofs, uprooted giant redwoods, and knocked down telephone poles. Our neighbors sandbagged their doorways and garages. Every day, Kirk and I peered out our bedroom window and uttered heathen prayers for the oak tree to stay upright. Its gnarled, curvy branches waved reassurance at us. Still, we worried.

Our arborist, who came by twice a year to marvel at its size and grace, also reassured us. "This oak has been through hundreds of storms," he said. "It will handle this weather."

He was right. By midwinter, our oak was still standing. But inside the house, the secret and mystery of Kirk's illness was taking a toll on our family. I was a wreck, pulling stress-induced all-nighters. He was crabby and in pain. The kids, now ten and thirteen, acted out, frequently fighting, biting their nails, having nightmares.

Kirk saw yet another doctor, this one at UCSF. The doc broke Kirk's clavicle open, scooped out the marrow, and ran the biopsy sample down to the lab. I paced in the waiting room and called my mom.

The doctor came out and put his hand on my knee. "I wish I had better news. It's cancer, but the test was inconclusive. There's no treatment."

Shortly after getting that biopsy result, Kirk and I planned a kid-free getaway to the Wine Country. As we packed on Friday morning, we glimpsed the tire swing hanging a little lower than usual. After so many weeks of rain, it was not surprising for the tire to fill with water. The nylon rope, several years old now, looked as if it had stretched an extra six inches. We wondered out loud if we should have someone take a look at our oak while we were gone. As we drove to our hotel, we debated. If the tire swing was lower, maybe the tree was sinking. Maybe we should have it radically trimmed, to reduce drag. Neither of us could relax. We checked in and holed up in our room. We hardly ate dinner that night, and sleep evaded us.

At dawn, Ethan, texted us a picture of the swing touching the ground. We flew into action, calling an emergency tree specialist. We texted the babysitter and neighbors to keep kids and pets out of the backyard. The arborist was at our house within two hours. He said the tree looked healthy and there was no imminent threat of it failing, but until someone trimmed it, people should not use their backyards. We rested easier knowing the oak was safe for now, and forced ourselves out for a drive in the Wine Country. But the scenery was lost on us. Our hearts wanted to be home.

We'd just returned to our hotel when my cell rang. It was the babysitter. She screamed, "Your tree fell down!"

In the background, I heard Ethan keening, hysterically shrieking, "No! No! The tree!" I imagined my son, pinned under the oak. I pictured the limbs crushing our house and the neighbors' house next door.

I screamed at Kirk, "The oak tree fell!"

In a blur, we sped home through the rain. Ethan was fine, but shaken. He had been standing at the window in the family room at the back of our house for hours, watching the tree sink into the ground, and saw it as it fell. Mercifully, its huge limbs had missed him and our family room by a few feet and missed the neighbors' house by inches, crashing through our shared fence and flattening their trampoline. It was a miracle that nobody was killed.

We stared out the family room window. The glorious oak now lay on its side like some alien life form with giant veins stretching up in the air.

That night, I lay on my side in bed, facing the window to the backyard. I started to sob. I told Kirk that we could stand to be more like the oak tree. We should be good to our environment. We should bring others happiness. We should live a long life. When we die, we should give a gentle warning of our upcoming departure. And when we go, we should do as little damage as possible. He sighed and patted my hand. I couldn't believe he could be so stoic during such an emotional time. But I should have known by then that he was much like an oak tree himself.

For months, I had seen Kirk appear to be healthy, just like my majestic tree. Experts have remained positive, but like the tire swing hanging too low on the oak, the pain in Kirk's shoulder is a reminder of the fine line between health and death. Feeling guilty for my anger, I tell myself to enjoy the time that I have with my husband, to love him as an essential part of my home and heart, just as I loved my tree. Frequently, I find myself wondering if there was anything I could have done to save it. And if Kirk should be doing more to save himself.

The reality is that everything dies eventually, as Mother Nature dictates. Kirk is a medical mystery. How can someone with cancerous tumors throughout his body continue to ski, race cars, walk the dog, make love? How can he seem to be okay with this situation when it is destroying me?

I will always marvel at his height, his bravery, and his strength. Like our oak, Kirk may be fortunate to live a long life. Long enough to stretch out to his family like the wide branches of a valley oak that provide shelter to birds. To weather the seasons of fair and foul weather. To dig his roots deep into the soil around him, even if the ground is shaky, and to hold on.

Mindy Uhrlaub is the author of the novel *Unnatural Resources* and wrote and produced the feature film *STALLED*. She is also a former *PULP* magazine music reviewer and copyeditor. Mindy plays keyboards in the band 40th Day, which toured with Kansas and performed with The Smashing Pumpkins. Her writing appears in the anthology *Mamas Write* and she has performed her work at San Francisco's Lit Crawl.

MOVING ON

Rupture and Reconciliation

Lorrie Goldin

Sharon and I met in the dining hall at college, our plastic trays overflowing with carbohydrates served up by squat matrons in hairnets. She had skin-tight white pants, bouncy blonde curls, and aviator glasses framing green eyes arched in a perpetual startle. Sharon had been a geeky nerd in high school, like most of us at our ivy-clad college. But she was a California exotic next to my New England wallflower. We had the same coloring, yet it looked much better on her.

Sharon poked me in the stomach, giggling that I reminded her of her mother. "You're so soft and squooshy—pear-shaped, just like her!" she exclaimed. Sharon was clearly fond of her mother, so I forgave the insult. It wouldn't be the last time.

Sharon did her homework before agreeing to be room-mates the following year—she asked mutual acquaintances if I was boring. ("Most of them said, 'Only a little,'" Sharon told me as we threw our names into the housing lottery together.) I was less rigorous. That this charismatic Californian liked me was enough. She knew all the lyrics to songs and appraised men by pronouncing, "He makes me cream in my pants." That's how I felt about the guy who lived upstairs. But he chose Sharon over me, and I swallowed my disappointment. Such a preference seemed the natural order, and I grew accustomed to accepting my place in it. It didn't really matter, as long as Sharon welcomed me into her radiant orbit.

After we graduated, I spent the summer avoiding my future in my parents' basement. Sharon lived three time zones away with her own family. We spent a lot of time on the phone. "Why don't you come out to California?" Sharon proposed one night.

Since it was the only idea all summer that made me smile, I soon boarded a Greyhound bus, waving good-bye to my stunned parents.

Sharon and I shared an apartment and found low-wage jobs. We lived on Top Ramen served in cast-off melamine donated by her mother. After saving and scrimping our pennies for a year, we traveled abroad, spending nearly every minute together for four months, except when flirtations lengthened into one-night stands.

Sharon took excellent care of me. She chased away pickpockets I mistook for sweet children outside the Colosseum. She ran reconnaissance missions to check out the cute guys next door in our Santorini hotel. In a moment of unparalleled altruism, she even went for the one we thought might be gay because I preferred his friend.

One night, after gorging on unwashed strawberries from an open-air market, I erupted from both ends of my body. Sharon cleaned up the stinking mess. She murmured softly and pressed cool washcloths to my forehead. I had not been so tenderly cared for since childhood.

Just as I reminded Sharon of her mother, she reminded me of mine. It wasn't a physical resemblance that felt so familiar, but the promise of another mutual adoration society. My mother taught me bawdy drinking songs as she ironed, letting me sprinkle the rumpled clothes with water from the perforated top of an old soda bottle while we sang and chatted for hours. Even the ordinary was magical under the spell of being together.

So it was with Sharon and me. We chortled endlessly over in-jokes, reveling in each other's cleverness. I loved the feeling of being inside each other's skin, of recreating the blissful and safe cocoon I'd inhabited with my mother as we talked about everything and nothing.

Then a man came between us.

It was Thanksgiving, one of those first heady feasts away from family when we experimented with making our own traditions. I was eager to introduce Sharon to Keith, the guy I barely thought of as my boyfriend since all we did was sleep together. I looked forward to the withering critiques my best friend and I would surely make of him later.

"You should sleep with him, too!" I proposed. Keith would be just a plaything, like a catnip mouse two cats bat back and forth.

The introductions went better than expected. After dinner, all three of us lay atop my turquoise-flowered Indian bedspread, tipsy, giggling, and flirting. Keith lay between me and Sharon, our arms and legs a jumble. Sharon reached across Keith's chest, stroking both of us. I reached back, warm and buzzed. Suddenly, cold sobriety descended. What the hell was I doing? I pulled away and spent the night frozen, sleepless, and alone in my bed after Sharon and Keith moved to the floor, pulling all the blankets with them.

Having handed Keith to Sharon on a Thanksgiving platter, a few days later I wanted him back.

"But you said it was okay!" Sharon protested.

"Well, I've changed my mind," I said.

After agreeing to cool it, they saw each other behind my back. When I found out, I was furious. "You lied to me!" I raged as Sharon sputtered.

We didn't speak for more than two years. It's not that Sharon got the man I wanted. It's that she chose Keith over me.

Underneath my hurt and anger, I missed Sharon, especially after she moved abroad and her relationship with Keith was put on hold. She must have missed me too—our conciliatory aerogrammes crossed in the mail. "Hey, thinking of you," we each wrote from opposite sides of the Pacific Ocean. Just like that, we were best friends again.

A few years later, the tension began to mount again. It may have been that I started to become the tortoise to her hare in our romantic contests. I met the man I would later marry. When he and I bought a house, Sharon sniffed, "How incredibly bourgeois." A similar insult infused her congratulations when we became engaged. As my maid of honor, Sharon was late to the wedding and called me a Nazi for being uptight. When my daughter was born, Sharon swooped in with cuddles for her and snide jokes for me and my husband about how insufferable parenthood had made us. As she continued to layer together incredible warmth and hostility, I continued to eat it up without quite realizing that I was ingesting poison. After all, snarkiness was just part of our secret language.

Perhaps Sharon was threatened as I surpassed her in the marriage and motherhood race. But that is only part of it. I, too, was threatened by her expanding world. Sharon traveled all over Japan and Europe while I tended my nest. She was flamboyant, alive, mercurial, while I was quieter, constant, smug. She was a better talker. I was a better listener. I should have spoken up more, and sooner, like a true friend. Instead, over coffee one day, I ambushed her with a self-righteous blast, saying I was sick of her constant digs and jealousy and wanted nothing more to do with her.

"Jealous of *you?*" Sharon retorted. "Don't be ridiculous."

This time, no letters crossed in the mail.

A decade and a half since we'd met at college, and years after that last rupture, Sharon and I bumped into one another at a mutual friend's wedding.

"Fancy meeting you here!" she exclaimed. "Remember Keith?"

I took it all in: her billowing belly, her husband—the man

I'd introduced her to—emerging from the bar carrying drinks. Beer for him, sparkling water for Sharon; she was hugely pregnant with their first child.

"Congratulations," I stammered, scanning the garden for hedges to hide behind.

But it was too late. Sharon took my arm in hers and begged my husband and me to sit with them, saying, "You can coach me if I go into labor!"

Despite her bulk, she was the most elegant guest there. And, of course, the most fun. We clicked again, like always. But we made no plans to keep in touch.

Two years later, I nearly crashed my shopping cart into Sharon's in Safeway's produce aisle. It was too late to duck behind the avocado bin. Her curly-headed toddler watched from the seat as we exchanged awkward greetings. The requisite clucking over her cherubic son helped us find our groove. Within a few minutes, we'd eased into our usual patter as if days, not years, had gone by.

Sharon and I are in our sixties now. We see each other every couple of months for lunch or a walk. We are no longer young women who yearn to find a replacement for the mothers we miss, but mothers of children who are now older than we were when we met. Sharon is still charismatic, and I am still only a little bit boring. We still revel in each other's cleverness. Our friendship is perhaps more distant, but also more sane.

Today, Sharon is late for our lunch date. As I stand waiting on the corner, I see her far away in the next block, stopped in front of a garden. She bends over gently toward each luscious rose, drinking in the scent, caressing the petals. I watch, surprised and touched by the loveliness of her private self. I am more familiar with my flamboyant friend whose spark has so long enticed and burned me. I'd like to get to know this other woman too—the one who stops to smell the roses. Then I realize she's been there all along, waiting for me to see her.

Lorrie Goldin is a psychotherapist and writer in the San Francisco Bay Area. Her work has appeared in a variety of venues, including *Salon*, the *Washington Post*, and KQED's *Perspectives*. She blogs at *Shrinkrapped*.

Struck by Lightning

Terry McQueen

"Any relation to Steve McQueen?" is a question I'm often asked. I used to smile and answer, "I wish." Then I'd come back with, "No, not Steve, another famous McQueen. It's a long story."

I met my husband, Glenn McQueen, at my first computer animation job in the early '90s. He was a high-energy, uber-talented animator, a Canadian expat living in the Bay Area. I had also moved, from LA, to join this young, hip, tiny company. My limited contact with Glenn at work—mostly short conversations confirming his progress on a TV commercial—jangled my nerves. Talented people scared me. But fast-forward fifteen months and we were dating. Less than two years later, we tag-teamed over to Pixar.

The rough-edged, motorcycle-riding, sports-car-loving goofball was also a softie who rolled around on the floor with any puppy he came across, drove thirty miles to my house to pick up my makeup when I'd stay over on a work night, and possessed the most authentic values of any man I'd ever met.

I proudly took his last name when we married. This was a time of hyphenates, men taking their wives' last names, or women choosing to keep their own. His last name was cool, it was colorful. I wasn't crazy about mine, "Herrmann," and having to repeat "that's two r's and two n's" when someone tripped over the spelling.

Soon, another little McQueen entered the world—our daughter, Kate. She had my long legs and his impish personality, even as a toddler. We were in for a ride.

Pixar was an intense period of our lives. I spent my time with production charts and schedules, while Glenn honed his artistic skills and became one of the most skilled animators in the company. He claimed to have the best job on the planet and thanked the heavens daily, even though he was an atheist. We shared the thrill of working on the first *Toy Story*, riding along with the company as they began to dominate the animation world. I was a proud wife when he was promoted to Supervising Animator on the next three Pixar films, and his success allowed me to stay at home with Katie when she was a toddler. New parenthood was jarring, but we were happy, and the road ahead appeared to be all clear.

A few years later, Glenn was working at his peak of commitment but wearing himself down. He was tired, he looked pale, he had a few unusual bouts of the flu. When a lump appeared on his shoulder, my heart imploded. He was too busy to get it checked out. Within a couple of weeks, two more appeared, followed by a baseball-size black bruise under his arm. We didn't know what we didn't know. Initial testing was negative, but outpatient surgery to remove the growths crashed us into the world of cancer. Metastatic melanoma.

The next eleven months were a blur of hospitals, surgery, useless chemotherapy, and too many tests. There was never any good news. Glenn's goal was to live long enough to see Katie graduate from high school; his second wish was to return to Pixar and the "normal" work life he treasured. He was deep in pre-production on the movie *Cars*, more in his element that he'd ever been.

In the last month of Glenn's life, I set up home base in the corner of his hospital room on a scuffed green vinyl lounger that became my cramped sleeping quarters. It was October, and in my corner I could turn my head to the left and watch the love of my life slowly disappear, or to the right, where the red and gold oak leaves became more saturated each day, the sun shifting lower in the sky, the mood more ruddy, darker, as October dragged on. It would never again be my favorite month.

In what had become an alternate universe, Pixar kept on plugging away on *Cars*. Glenn's work buddies came by to catch him up on the latest developments, everyone pretending that he'd be back to work soon. The movie's main character had become reminiscent of a sturdy American muscle car—Mustang-style, bright red.

Director and Pixar demigod John Lasseter came to the hospital a few times. John had the power to change anything at anytime. It was a remarkable thing to witness at work, but I wish he could've changed *our* storyline too. When John came in the hospital room for his last visit with Glenn, I was dipping a washcloth into a bowl of ice water, wringing it out, and gently placing it on his forehead while his fever continued to internally combust his body. The diorama in that room was not the world the three of us normally inhabited, one of friendship, fun, fantasy, and creativity—a world where scenes like these could be deleted, fixed, improved, or never even drawn in the first place.

Glenn wobbled in and out of consciousness while his boss and mentor kept up a conversation that wasn't likely to be heard by anyone but me. I continued dipping, wringing, and wiping. And then John gave my husband a true gift, and me a promise of something real in the future: Pixar was going to name the star of the movie after Glenn. The bright and shiny red race car would be called McQueen.

Fast-forward four years to the movie release and the intro-duction of the newest McQueen, Lightning. Six boxes of radio-controlled character cars, plush toys, DVDs, books, and action figures arrived for Katie and me from Pixar. Along with my husband's namesake character came a sensory onslaught of billboards, bus signs, and TV commercials that blared that name—*my* name, *his* name. My seven-year-old daughter's after-noon ritual of watching the Disney Channel opened her young eyes to her new celebrity. Stirring spaghetti in the kitchen, my heart alternately rose and fell with conflicting emotions.

One day, as I blithely entered a Target, I encountered blasts of bright, shiny red cars everywhere—toys, games, bedsheets, pillows, T-shirts. The crazy, amped eyes of McQueen, strangely like Glenn's, followed me from every angle. I nearly doubled over with laughter upon spotting a Lighting McQueen musical potty-training seat. It would've been a perfect addition to his office decor, nailed to his door and rigged to open and close while greeting his guests with a recording of his voice. And I couldn't call to tell him what I'd found.

I was invited to the speedway in Charlotte for the *Cars* world premiere. It was not ironic that the outdoor screening took place during a powerful thunder and lightning storm, soaking the red carpet. A photo op with Owen Wilson, who visibly squirmed when the producer reminded him I was "the wife," a cocktail party with comedian Larry the Cable Guy. Coworkers and friends treated me gingerly, kept an eye out for me, making sure I had a plate of barbecue to go with my vodka, and possibly worried that I'd start to cry. The energy of the occasion was a high, but Glenn should've been there. Was his spirit making itself heard through the lightning in the sky?

Lightning in nature is unpredictable; it flashes in a moment, then ghosts before it disappears. There's such a small chance you'll be struck by lightning that you never think it'll happen to you.

⁓

It's been eleven years now since Lighting McQueen became a public figure, and two more movies have embedded the character into the brains of children worldwide. I haven't been able to bring myself to see either one. The second film came out five years after the first, and we didn't receive any more toys or party invitations. I was happy that the McQueen name was continuing on in pop culture, and nine years after Glenn's passing, I was proving I could "do life," but I was miffed that the "novelty" of his death was wearing off. And to me, it seemed that we were forgotten

By the third incarnation of *Cars*, internet chatter was wondering, *Why do they keep making these movies? Is the character still relevant?* In the film, Lightning is dealing with aging, which is more than relevant in my life. The race car is slowing down, getting saggy, fading. But inside, he feels like the young upstart he once was.

I'm not that cocky, but I can relate. Years go by, and Glenn is moving further away from my everyday thoughts, but it's hard to face the fact that I'm aging without him. He's forever forty-one, but my body, my transmission, is running down. Being alone without him beside me is like forever driving your car with the small spare tire from the trunk—your forward motion is hindered, wobbly, you can't safely go over fifty-five.

⁓

Even though it's been a long time now, I'm still caught off guard when I see a small child struggling to drag his Lightning McQueen suitcase behind him in a crowded airport. In the past, I'd blurt out, "Hey, let me show you my keychain, my McQueen car!" and offer a brief backstory. Now, I just smile to myself and stay quiet. These days I just want to keep these treasured memories private. And if I'm ever asked if I'm related to Steve, I shake my head and shrug. Some of the world may know the story, but I no longer feel the need to share it with everyone I meet.

Terry McQueen is a writer, baker, animal lover, and Golden State Warriors fan. A former Pixar production manager, she is currently working on a memoir about her late husband, Glenn "Lightning" McQueen, and her life as a solo parent. She lives in Oakland, California, with her daughter and several spoiled pets.

On Being a Girl

Nina Vincent

I was forty-three years old before I felt ready to parent a girl. When I was pregnant at thirty with my first child, I prayed that he would be a boy. A boy felt safer. I wouldn't have to worry that I would wound my girl child with the messages that my mother had drilled into me about girls being too sensitive, too manipulative, too provocative, and too feminine.

Raised on a farm in New Jersey, my mother carried out the duties of a farmer—chopping heads off the chickens and milking cows. Makeup and frilly dresses were for "sissies" in my mother's world. My mother's skirts did not flow or swirl; they stood stiff around her busy legs and never came low enough to leave the shoes on her feet a mystery.

My mother was a strong, capable woman who raised the three of us on her own after my father's death when I was ten years old and my brothers were six and fourteen. She loathed whining, weakness, and pettiness. She forbade me to get my ears pierced, even in high school, and hated the fact that my best friend in ninth grade was a southern belle who painted my face with baby blue eye shadow, thick black mascara, and pink lip gloss. These things said "slut," "hussy," and "girlie" to my mother. Perhaps she was hoping to protect me from a society that still valued women and girls for their looks rather than the content of their character, but to me her criticism was the butcher's knife that filleted layers of my self-esteem.

It wasn't until I became pregnant with my son that I began to feel the wonders of being a woman. When Eli was born and latched on to my breasts, where he happily suckled and drew comfort, I marveled at being a woman for the first time in my life. I saw my body not as an object to be admired or critiqued by the male world, or criticized by my mother, but rather as a miracle that had carried, and now nourished, my child.

When Eli turned eleven and his increasing desire for independence took him farther from my arms, I began to dream of having another child. The yearning I had to adopt a girl had taken seed in my heart and would not let go. Confident that I'd fully healed from my childhood wounds, I was eager to raise a daughter.

When it came time to find a name for our baby, who for eight months had to wait in an orphanage in Guatemala City while the bureaucracy finished dotting its i's and crossing its t's, I discovered the name Amalia. My son wanted to give his sister a name with nickname potential. For the year it took to bring Amalia home, I had carried a jade stone whose shape looked to me like a mother holding her child. So Jade gave Amalia the nickname potential my son wished for. Amalia Jade—AJ.

As soon as we chose her name, I felt the excitement of having a baby girl in my life. Amalia would wear dresses if she liked, and even small amounts of makeup. I would allow her to pierce her ears at seven or eight. I was fully prepared to embrace all things "girl" in my daughter, and to instill a sense of pride in her. I would teach her how to be strong in a world that still puts women at the back end of the line. I would tell her that she could be whomever she chose to be in life, and that through education, determination, kindness, and wit she would find her place. I was determined to raise her as independent. She would wear pants or a dress, hold a hammer or lipstick. Above all, she would not grow up being ashamed of who she was.

As my baby grew and her hair tickled the tops of her shoulders where the straps of her pink and yellow dresses highlighted the beauty of her brown skin, I sought to enrich her world with a growing sense of sisterhood.

Our teachers come to us in different forms throughout life. I'm well aware of the ways in which our children help us grow and expand beyond places of comfort and knowing. I'm certain I wasn't prepared for the ways in which Amalia Jade would demand that I stretch. I was unaware of how many little boxes my mind inhabited, and how clumsy I would be climbing out of each and every one of them.

Amalia's need to control the world around her interfered with her ability to be flexible. She couldn't hear the needs of others, and at school she struggled socially and was unable to navigate the rules of friendship, especially with other girls. So, Amalia started playing kickball with the boys at recess. She'd come home happy to have had success with others on the playing field. There was bickering and disagreement, of course, but Amalia was better able to handle the banter of boys than the complex and subtle intricacies of relationships among girls. The cruelties she'd experienced with several of her female classmates had left deeper scars in her psyche than I'd realized. So, when she said to me one day while brushing her teeth, our reflections speaking to one another in the mirror, "Mama, maybe it would be easier if I were a boy," I didn't give it much attention. I responded with logic. "You don't need to be a boy to play with the boys."

But slowly, Amalia began to choose the boys' hand-me-down clothes in her dresser over the girls'. It wasn't uncommon for me to hear, "Should I dress like a boy or a girl today,

Mama?"—to which I, the evolved mother, responded, "Whichever you like. What do you feel like?"

I heard my ten-year-old child ask for a boy's haircut, but I didn't hear the desperation and confusion she felt with all her failed attempts at friendship. She'd never definitively said to me, "I want to be a boy." It wasn't until we were away at adoption family camp the summer of her tenth year and she broke down in an anxious fit of rage over my packing choices—I had brought her bright purple and pink bathing suit rather than her trunks and swim shirt—that I detected something different in my child's need to look like a boy.

While Amalia Jade spent time in her camp group during the day, I attended various seminars provided for parents of transracial adoptive families. One of the speakers that day was a Latina woman who spoke about transgender people and gave a presentation, with tables and charts, explaining the proper terminology for the various different places on the gender spectrum. Those charts stared back at us while the speaker began to tell me things about my child that I had never considered. Forty percent of transgender people attempt suicide. Forty percent. We can't know what drives them to take their own lives, but there's a good chance that for some at least, not being seen, accepted, and supported by family and friends contributes to their pain and suffering.

I knew the pain that comes when someone you trust shames you for being the only person you know how to be. I'd grown up hiding my femininity behind large windbreakers and a tough veneer. I left that seminar knowing I would make sure the pattern of shaming didn't continue.

I fetched Amalia from her group, and as we walked back to our room, with an afternoon allotted for family free time, I asked her, "Do you still want that boy's haircut you've been asking about?"

Amalia looked into my eyes and answered with an emphatic, "Yes."

"Get the picture of what you want and we'll bring it into the hair clinic."

My child gave me a side hug, and a smile that forged a cavern across her face. "Thank you, Mama," she said. "You really understand me."

In that moment, I knew that I was not only saving my child from the pain of being judged by her mother, I was also healing the wounds that were still buried deep beneath my own skin.

And so, Amalia Jade became AJ. Although my twelve-year-old identifies as he, and has become my son, he is still, in many ways, very much the child I dreamed he would be. He is bright, energetic, and fierce. He loves to sing. This year, AJ joined the boys' choir. At their big performance, he stood so proudly beside his buddies on the stage, his black tuxedo crisp and clean.

I often laugh with friends and say I was destined to raise boys and live with men all around me. Sometimes, though, I'm sad that I'm not getting to raise that strong, smart, powerful woman I'd dreamed of raising this time around. But honestly, raising AJ isn't all that different from raising Amalia Jade. He is loyal and kind, empathic and smart. He is everything I'd hoped my daughter would be.

Nina Vincent is the mother to step and birth sons, and one child born in Guatemala. Her articles on transracial adoption have been published in *Adoption Today*, *Adoption Mosaic*, *Adoptive Families Magazine*, and *Adoption Voices Magazine*, and she was also a 2016 Listen to Your Mother San Francisco cast member. She is the author of the debut YA novel *Sliding Into Home*. Nina's writing is inspired by her work with street children in Oaxaca, Mexico, and in group home settings in the United States.

Family Trees

Laurel K. Hilton

Thirty-five years later, I still remember how the smell of the sawdust and glue in the woodshop mingled with the scent of the fresh pines and maple outside. I was nine years old, visiting my grandparents in the North Woods of Michigan. Down a dark, narrow aisle—past rocking chairs, stools, and animal carvings—there, towering above me, was a mysterious pointy shape covered by a large oilcloth.

The woodshop owner, an elderly man, whisked off the cover, and I peered through my thick, fringed bangs to see the most magnificent sight: a handmade, three-story dollhouse. A glazed, butter-yellow tile chimney snaked up one side of the house, emblazoned with a bright orange monogrammed "M" for Munson, my last name. Turning the house 180 degrees, the cutaway view revealed tiny wooden chairs, sofas, lamps, and a bunk bed with miniature pink gingham mattresses, all custom-made. It was breathtaking, and it was for me—a magical house to fill with my love and imagination.

That summer, the dollhouse, wedged into the back of my parents' car, traveled with me nearly 2,300 miles back to my home in California, where I played with it well into my early teens.

My family's roots in Michigan's Upper Peninsula run deep. Our ancestors arrived in this remote region in the early 1860s as the Civil War played out to the east and south. Old newspaper clippings mark my great-grandfather as the first settler's son born in Republic Township. His brother, my great-uncle, discovered a half-buried axe handle in a nearby creek bed dating back to the Vikings and Leif Eriksson. A riverfront parcel is named Munson Park after my grandfather; half the headstones in the cemetery are Munson relatives. For over 150 years, my family has been a part of this town.

Even though I grew up in California, I spent every other summer in Republic. I learned to fish, splashed around in the tangy, iron ore–rich Michigamme River, explored abandoned mines and ghostly, deserted hotels with my brother, and watched my grandparents bury two beloved pet dogs in the orchard behind their home. My grandmother and I collected wild raspberries, which we turned into pies and jam. Even now, I remember the sweet taste of berry jam rolling around on my tongue. My brother and I helped my grandfather cut the grass surrounding our family tombstones and lay wildflowers at their bases. We watched our nearly eighty-year-old grandfather flirt with other longtime residents, old school chums—women also in their seventies and eighties, but to him still girls in frocks and braids.

Before me, my dad and his siblings swam in the Michigamme, and before him, my grandfather Munson, and before him, my great-grandfather Munson. Someday, I knew, I would bring my own children to swim and experience all the wonderful things I had learned in Republic as a kid. My girls were six and nine—close to the age I had been when I first visited the town. It was time to plan that trip.

But then the rug was ripped out from under me. After years of difficult long-distance upkeep from over two thousand miles away, my dad, the trustee of my grandparents' estate, had begun to sell off pieces of the family land in Republic. Not realizing I would care, he did not tell me until only one parcel was left. He may not have even planned to ever tell me. But I happened to mention one evening over a late-summer dinner on his Southern California patio that I was ready to take my kids for a visit. "Oh, why would you do that?" he asked. "I've already sold nearly all the family property."

What. The. Fuck.

Tears sprang to the corners of my eyes. I dropped my fork, looked down into my lap, and swallowed hard. I went flush and tingled cold seemingly all at once. It didn't help that he was oblivious to the pain this devastating news had caused.

I whimpered audibly, then became angry and indignant. "Why wasn't I consulted? Aren't I a Munson too!? Why can't I take over the financial support of the property, at least for the one parcel you haven't sold?"

He found this a ridiculous proposition. He didn't think I could handle it—me, now a middle-aged woman with a family of my own. And he didn't understand my sentimentality for a place I hadn't been born and had spent only parts of my child-hood summers.

Was I trying too hard to live in the past, in memories? No.

Resolute, I told my dad that we would visit Republic together one more time and walk down memory lane—mine and his. I would bring my kids. He could come or not, but I was going. To my surprise, he agreed to go.

We planned our trip for that fall, and by the time we arrived, my dad had sold the last of our private property. All that remained in our care was the riverfront park. It is a beautiful, grassy bluff overlooking the Michigamme River, placed in the very spot where my great-grandparents' first home in town once stood—a home long gone, unwillingly sold by Great-Grandpa Charlie Munson in the 1960s to the local mining company and blasted away like many others at the time. Now the land was returned to nature, re-purchased by my family and gifted to the town with us as caretakers.

The first thing my kids did at Munson Park was scrabble over the granite memorial that had my family history inscribed on it. Then they rolled down the grassy slope nearly into the chilly river. My ancestors would have been so delighted with their exuberance.

After visiting the park, we drove to another area of town and down a gravel lane dotted with small cabins and one large home, literally my own memory lane. All of the land and homes had belonged to my grandparents; now they'd been sold, in pieces, to new owners. We arrived at the big house and, after knocking on the front door several times to no answer, I grabbed my kids and hurried down toward the river, reasoning with myself that this place had been in our family much longer than the new tenants who had owned it less than six months. If they showed up, I would do my best to charm them. My dad stayed in the idling car. He wasn't taking any chances.

Looking across the river, I sighed happily. There was the same island I had rowed to countless times with my brother. It seemed so much smaller now. The white birch trees on the other side were reflected in the water, painting a picture of soft greens, dazzling oranges, and brilliant yellows. It took my breath away, and goose bumps rippled along my arms and back. I smiled until it hurt.

We dashed down the stairs and out to the dock where I had fished as a kid, sometimes even in the pouring rain because the fish took your line better in the rain. Then we walked through the orchard and admired the mossy headstones where my grandparents had buried their dogs so long ago. My youngest daughter jumped on the tire swing hanging nearby and I snapped a quick photo.

I could have stayed all afternoon, gazing at the white birch trees and losing myself in memories. As we left, I quickly peered in the window of the cozy living room and adjoining kitchen. There was my grandfather's old poker table, the rickety ladder leading up to the loft where I had hid out during thunderstorms.

New to me were wood sculptures made of white birch perched over the fireplace and, on the wall, a hand-painted sign that read "Welcome to Our Home." I smiled. The house and the land were still loved.

~~~

After returning to California, I went looking for the old doll-house, the one my grandparents had commissioned for me over thirty years ago. I found it resting on the eaves of my parents' attic. The dollhouse was a little mildewed and dusty, but still in one piece. The faint smell of the woodshop and Michigan's North Woods came back to me. Not every piece of my family history in Republic had been sold.

Soon I will wedge the butter-yellow dollhouse mono-grammed with the bright orange "M" into the back of my Highlander and drive the 500 miles from my parents' home to deliver it to its new owners, my daughters.

Laurel K. Hilton is an author featured in two previous anthologies—*Mamas Write* and *Nothing But The Truth: 73 Women on Life's Transitions*. Her writing has also appeared in *Sonoma Magazine*, *Mill Valley Herald*, *Parents Press*, and the Denver-based *Examiner*. She lives with her family in Northern California.

The Right Fit

Meghen Kurtzig

One Sunday morning I called my mother. This was not an every-Sunday kind of a thing. I had something to tell her, and I was jittery, which could have been due to my coffee addiction, but that's a confession that can wait for another day. She was probably standing in the kitchen holding the receiver of the wall phone, the spiral cord bouncing as she squinted at the paper calendar on the cork board, looking to see when I was scheduled for my next visit across the country.

I took a deep breath and told her the news.

"Mom, I have decided to . . . umm . . . to become a writer!" I exhaled and waited for the long sigh, the questions, the confusion.

A second of silence and then she said, "Of course," like it was just another day. Not the day I revealed my dark secret.

After all, I had spent three years in graduate school for nursing, not writing. The four years before that had been spent trying to follow my parents' conflicting advice. *Do what you love*, my mother encouraged, while my father steered me to *go where the money is*.

Being a dutiful daughter, I tried to combine both pieces of guidance during my early years of college. I took my interest in science and my love of swimming and combined it into a major in marine biology. I imagined a tropical life training dolphins and relaxing on the beach. The reality looked more like standing waist-deep in the cold ocean counting barnacles on a pier piling. It wasn't love, and I didn't stick around long enough to see a paycheck.

So I dropped the "marine" and stuck with biology. Looking distractingly sexy in my white lab coat and safety goggles, I spent my days hunched over dead creatures with my anatomy lab partners. I enjoyed digging for ligaments and obscure nerves, though the formaldehyde fumes made me feel like I was suffocating inside a jar of pickles and will be forever seared into my nostrils. Physiology had me putting bodies—mine and unsuspecting frogs'—through tests to slow heart rates and test renal function. We drank can after can of soda to see if the sodium benzoate made us need to pee (the answer is yes), and I learned the benefits of quick-untie scrub pants.

As my college days came to an end, the question remained: What was I going to do with this degree? Medicine was the obvious answer. It certainly had the cash flow piece to satisfy Dad. But I wasn't feeling the love, and I wasn't sure why. Maybe I was still holding out for that tropical life on the beach.

So I explored nursing. The world needed nurses, and I could use science and still get paid enough to survive in San Francisco, where there is a beach but decidedly *not* tropical temperatures. What San Francisco lacked in warmth it made up for in serendipity. I found myself married and in the city to stay.

However, when I stepped into nursing, it felt like a pair of pants that you put on right after the holidays. You know they are supposed to fit, but you can't quite get them buttoned. You can make it work if you squeeze a little here and tug a little there, but you're never really comfortable.

In spite of all my contortions, nursing just wasn't right—but I couldn't tell why. I only saw the fire in my classmates as they followed their calling and the lack of fire in me as I slogged through my coursework.

After graduation and two children, I gave up the fight with the nursing pants and moved on to maternity pants. The yoga pants years promptly followed. Much of it was a blur—little sleep, lots of *sand* . . . not the beautiful beach kind but the gritty, dirty, "I think I brought home the whole sandbox in my shoes" kind. Sometimes sleep-deprived memory loss can be a good thing.

Once the early parenting fog cleared, I decided that yoga pants were practical but lacked polish. I shopped around the nursing world looking for a job that would fit my new mama lifestyle, yet nothing seemed right. So I started spending time with my local mothers' club in an effort to begin a project on my own. But instead of gathering data on maternal/child health from the group as I had intended, I found myself sitting at a high-top table in Peet's Coffee across from the blonde and bespectacled editor-in-chief of the club's magazine. She offered me the job of writer and editor. After making sure she understood that I had no idea what I was doing, I got to work.

That's when it happened. The swooning, the heart palpitations, the giddy, can't-stop-smiling feeling. My team of staff writers sent articles, and I got lost in them, moving words around, whittling them down. The exciting treasure hunt of finding the perfect photo to go with the articles. The satisfaction of sending them off in a file to the printer and seeing the whole collection come together in thick, glossy splendor. When I didn't have an article that fit I had to write my own. I loved the thrill of the deadline, the challenge to make it happen. Who needed an emergency room for excitement when I had *words?*

Turned out, Mom was right. I was doing what I loved. Sorry, Dad—the chance of a hefty paycheck was slim.

In an effort to take this new relationship with writing to the next level, I attempted fiction. I love to read, especially novels, and I had an idea for a story. What could be so hard? I signed up for National Novel Writing Month (NaNoWriMo), which requires writing a draft of an entire novel in one month. When the month was up I was giddy, anticipating reading my brilliant creation. It was the novel everyone was going to want to read. But a closer look revealed that there was nothing brilliant about it. What I'd thought was plot sounded like rambling. My characters were cardboard and confused, my setting was flimsy and kept changing. Something was very wrong. The writing made me happy. I had found my calling. Why hadn't I created a masterpiece?

I'd thought I could go from reading books to creating them in one step. Like going from threading a needle to making Gucci couture in one month. But I didn't know how to write a novel any more than I knew how to sew a pair of pants. I needed a pattern and some lessons.

So I stocked up on books and I signed up for classes, which was the easy part. The hard part was the practice. The restraint of not wadding up and throwing a terrible draft in the trash. Instead, showing it to someone else, hoping that they didn't wad it up and toss it, at least not in front of my face.

Now, five years later, I'll admit there are days where I want to go running back to my lab coat and stethoscope. There are answers in science. There are tasks to accomplish. There is also a paycheck (kids to feed, you know). There are even days when I consider heading back into the freezing ocean (although not many)—those days when either the words don't come or they do but they sound worse than before. But even on my bad days, I keep the words flowing in my notebook or piling up on my laptop, no matter where my "desk" might be that day—often the inside of my crumb-filled car—because I am in love with this work. I am hooked on watching a scene develop from a murky idea to a clear picture and seeing my novel inch closer to something that I would like to pick up off a bookshelf and read.

So no, Mom and Dad, I'm not wearing the baggy scrubs I trained for, but I've found my new sense of style in my writer pants. Some days they are sweats, sometimes they are sleek and black, and even if occasionally I have to coax them on, I know I have found the right fit.

Meghen Kurtzig completed the Certificate Program in Novel Writing at Stanford University. She has read at Lit Crawl and her work can be found in *Talking River Review* and the anthology *Mamas Write*. She is currently working on novel revisions in the midst of parenting and traveling.

Burnt Toast

Christine Bent

There are so many ways to handle burnt toast. My husband eats it, even black. I toss it and start over. My mom? With five of us waiting, she scraped it and served it up as perfect, denying any burning whatsoever. That telltale burnt toast smell? "Old crumbs in the toaster!" she exclaimed. The dark sprinkles of charred residue on the bread? "Cinnamon toast!"

From scraping burnt toast to dressing up flat soda with a fancy tray, my mother's denial muscle was strong, and it flexed all through my childhood. This generated laughter and affectionate reminiscing among my siblings when we gathered years later. But when I became a mother myself, some of my formerly fond and even funny memories felt suddenly dangerous and scary in the context of parenting. I began to wonder: had my mother been aware of what she was denying, or simply living in ignorant bliss?

When I look back on one particular early memory through my mothering lens, the answer to this question takes on a new and almost urgent importance.

I was ten years old. Not ten and a half or almost eleven, which sounds closer to twelve and is when people might expect children to take on significant responsibilities, but just ten. I know this because my sister, my fourth sibling, was born on New Year's Eve, the day after my birthday. I already had three brothers, and when my favorite aunt and godmother—with whom I was staying—got the call, we joined hands and danced around the kitchen: "It's a girl! It's a *girl*!!" We twirled and jumped in glee.

She was *my* baby right from the start. I was always the first one up, and the one to greet her each morning. I scooped her out of the white lace bassinet where she waited quietly in the corner of our empty living room and laid her on the wicker changing table. There I put a fresh tiny diaper on her and chose a gown with ducks or bunnies or maybe clouds, then dressed and swaddled her. She resembled a mini bonbon straight out of a candy factory, and I cradled her in my arms as I walked to my parents' room. I handed her to my mother in bed for breastfeeding, then took her back again and walked, burped, and held her tight until school.

My grandmother had given me a fancy doll stroller from FAO Schwartz some years earlier. It was a miniature replica of a real English pram and came with two twin dolls with silky hair and real dresses. I hated dolls, so until my real live baby sister came along, that stroller only held stuffed animals. To my delight, a newborn six-pound baby fit perfectly in my doll stroller.

One evening, as she prepared dinner in our tiny galley kitchen while my brothers ran circles around the apartment and I held my baby sister, my mother suddenly exclaimed that we had nothing for dessert. She asked me if I would go out to buy custards.

It was 1975 in New York City, probably March, and I eagerly agreed. It went without saying that I would take my baby sister. I bundled her up, tucked her into my doll stroller, and pushed her out our apartment door. Just past the incinerator door, where our garbage tumbled down twelve floors and was magically burned into nothing, I pushed the button and rode our bright red elevator to the lobby. From there I headed out the heavy double locking doors and along a path that connected our building to the dozen or so that looked just like it. No doorman, no cell phone, just me and my baby sister. As darkness fell, I strolled past the vacant playground and basketball courts and out onto the sidewalk running east along 20th Street. I often walked this route to afternoon baseball practice on 16th Street in my Braves uniform and ponytail, but I was usually with my brothers or my dad.

I waited for the light and crossed the wide street to our neighborhood market, where we bought Yodels and Ring Dings or Sno Balls on our way home from baseball. I went straight to the counter, stood on my tippy toes to see the man over the top, and ordered six vanilla custards. I now think of these as crème brûlée, but back then they were just custards, sold in round ceramic dishes that you brought back later.

As I headed back out of the door with a fairly heavy brown bag rolled up at the top in one hand, pushing my baby sister with the other, a man kindly held the door open for me and smiled. Then, suddenly, his smile darkened and he exclaimed, "Oh my—she's real!" Followed quickly by, "How old are you? Are you with your mother?"

I proudly responded "Ten" and "No."

He stammered his surprise and received muttered affirmations from another patron entering the store, but I spun my stroller around and headed confidently for the crosswalk. I realized then that everyone else who had looked at me and smiled as I walked to the store must have thought I was pushing one of my fancy dolls with silk hair and real clothes, and that my mother must have been just up ahead, letting me pretend that I was a real big-girl mother.

That night, when my father came home from work, my family enjoyed the delicious vanilla custards for dessert. My mother bragged about how I was to thank, how I had gone all by myself with the baby to get them for her. I had never felt so proud.

After I became a mother, however, that pride morphed into disbelief. I couldn't stop thinking about the many possible turns of events that could have changed the outcome of that evening excursion. After years of wondering if it was really true, I finally asked my mother, hoping that I had remembered it wrong, that there was some crucial detail I'd missed—like our babysitter trailing me the whole time with my younger brothers, or my mother calling the storekeeper to look out and watch me cross the street. Or perhaps it really had been my doll in the stroller after all.

But my mother cheerfully confirmed that I did, in fact, take my infant sister out to buy custards, in my doll stroller, alone, on the Lower East Side of New York City one evening when I was ten. She sounded just as proud of me in retelling it as I remembered she had that night.

This led me to wonder not about the facts, which I had now come to accept, but about my mother's perspective. I had always assumed that on one level my mother was aware of the risks involved with some of her parenting decisions, but on another level simply denied them. In this case, I guessed, she had willed my outing to be routine, cute, and appropriate, overlooking the danger because worrying wasn't practical. The more I reflected on this as a parent, however, the more it began to feel like neglect. How could she put her two daughters at risk like that? And for dessert! It wasn't like she'd sent me for milk, or diapers.

Desperate for a different lens, I considered the possibility that my mother might not have actually been aware of the danger in that situation. Perhaps she imagined us back in the rural Wisconsin of her childhood, as if she were sending me over to the neighbor's farm to borrow some eggs? While that feels like a stretch, it does seem that her parenting was shaped by her idealistic, carefree upbringing. Fast-forward to raising five kids in Manhattan—a far cry from farm country, with no friendly neighbors or helpful husband—where my mother learned and practiced her most important survival skill: denial. If you practice something every day, it starts to become natural.

I wish my mother and I had the kind of relationship where we could speak deeply about parenting—or anything really.

Digging deep is very difficult; my mother is more comfortable on the surface, discussing the facts. And whether I like it or not, she is comfortable with the facts of this story. Which makes the prospect of probing deeper and questioning her perspective feel daunting, and even unkind. If I ask her what she was thinking—about whether she considered the possible dangers that evening—I worry she'd feel I was questioning her parenting, her judgment, perhaps even her love. And ultimately, I have enough opposing memories and experiences, highlighting years of devotion and sacrifice, to overcome those trace feelings of neglect.

More importantly, my mother now desperately counts on those memories to sustain her. Abruptly stricken with viral-induced dementia two years ago, she now rarely remembers recent conversations or details, yet her long-term memories of my childhood are intact. Her current slate is wiped clean every ten minutes—if you make a mistake and want to redo a conversation, it's truly possible.

At first, I thought this might present the perfect opportunity to delve deeper into her recollections of my upbringing and her parenting. Any pain my questioning might cause would be soon forgotten. But her denial muscle remains stubbornly strong. I can't even get her to admit that her clothes no longer fit—how can I hope to peel back the layers of stories that she's been comfortable with for fifty years? How can I expect her to acknowledge the burnt on the toast?

Breaking through the familiar surface of my mother's memories would be hard, painful work, and the last thing I want to do is cause her more suffering, even if just for ten minutes. These memories tether her to the past, a rock-solid base in the swirl of today's confusion. So instead of probing, I revel in our shared reminiscences; it's nice to have something we can enjoy and laugh about together, even if we stay on the surface. Seeing her face light up and her body relax into a fond memory reminds me how important it is to let her spend time where she feels comfortable. And how vital it is to help her hang on to these memories, even if they make me uneasy. Maybe I've learned how to embrace her version of cinnamon toast after all.

Christine Bent is a former sports writer and marketer who loves exploring the trails, farms, and waves of Marin County, California, with her three children and husband. She is a professional ski instructor and lifelong coach of youth sports ranging from ice hockey to lacrosse. When not adventuring with her family, tending her chickens, or caring for her mother, she writes about her free-range childhood in New York City.

Why Did the Moose Cross the Road?

Tarja Parssinen

There's a poem that hangs in my mother's house. I wrote it in college after returning from my first trip to Finland, so taken was I by a moose who crossed the highway just in front of us, forcing our car to a screeching stop. Over time, that moose became Finland for me: the beauty of the land and the power of finally meeting my grandfather's people.

You see, growing up one-quarter Finnish had always been the equivalent of being 100 percent Finnish. Not only was it easy to latch on to my grandfather's heritage, it was fun. For a kid who was looking for something, anything, to make her unique, I determined that the two little dots above the "a" in my last name—the umlaut of awesomeness—stood for *kick* and *ass*.[1]

Unlike most of my classmates with weird names who shrank in their seats during roll call, I sat even higher, proud that I was not just another Jen or Karen. When the confused

---

1. True, the umlaut got lost in the Parssinen emigration to America, but the ghost umlaut is there. Look closely.

teacher inevitably came to me, there would be a moment of silence—which I can only assume came from respect for the "j" in my name—followed, of course, by complete butchery. But this, too, was part of the performance; it then fell to me to speak my name correctly—a verbal pirouette, if you will. *"Tar-ya,"* I would say graciously. "The 'j' is like a 'y'."

I couldn't play volleyball, I didn't get invited to spin-the-bottle parties, I almost failed math in eighth grade, but by God, I was from the Arctic Circle! A land in which pasty skin is not only considered beautiful but also lauded as the new non-melanoma! A land where pickled herring are nestled lovingly amongst Marimekko tablecloths! Where the streets are paved with saunas, and reindeer are either kept as pets or eaten as snacks, I can't remember which.

I shrugged off my mother's heritage—a mutt mix of English, Irish, and Scottish—and put on my little fur-lined Finnish cape. Blonde-haired, blue-eyed, a natural inclination toward depression—I was ready to ride my heritage chariot as far as it would take me. Which, as luck would have it, was Finland.

It was the summer of 1998. I had just finished a semester abroad in Paris and my younger sister, Keija—*Kay-ya* (or *Ka-deeja*, as her sixth grade teacher called her)—came and joined me. Our plan was to travel around Europe and end the grand excursion in the land of our ancestors. We would stay with our cousin and visit our extended clan.

But the thing about being one-quarter Finnish is that Finland is the one place you don't feel Finnish at all. Keija and I were the American cousins who not only hated pickled herring for breakfast, but hated pickled herring at any time of day. Linguistic pickles, on the other hand, were right up our alley, and we became caught in one with our dear cousin Ensio, age seventy-five, almost immediately.

"Your name," Ensio told my sister, "has another meaning, a very rude meaning. I cannot call you by that name. I will call you by your middle name, Kaarina."

What in God's can of kipper fish snacks was Ensio talking about?

Let me explain. When my sister was born, my parents wanted a Finnish name. Eija was a popular name, as was Seija, so why not put a "K" in front and call her Keija? And that's the way my parents operate. No research, no call to the motherland to run it past them, just fly by the seat of your pants, which is super fun until you learn that you named your second-born daughter after a very old-fashioned colloquial word for "bedpan." Also called a "piss pot." Or a place where you did your business before the time of bathrooms.

Well, shit.

Nothing puts a damper on your first real trip to the land of your people like when your people refuse to say your name. Keija, fiery little soul that she is, would have none of it. She didn't endure twelve years of roll-call name butchery in school to have her Finnish name deleted entirely. She refused to answer to Kaarina. It was Piss Pot or nothing.

In the dichotomy of life, my visit to Finland was equal parts foreign and familiar. I didn't know my Finnish family, had never really spoken with them, and here they all were, direct relations—and reflections—of my grandfather, Johannes, that seventeen-year-old badass who had sailed across the sea in one of the last of the big schooners and started the line of American-born Parssinens.

Sometimes my trip to Finland was right out of Rick Steves: yes, there are, in fact, saunas in every house! Sometimes it was a truth you just couldn't fight: Finnish food sucks. And sometimes, expectations were left unfulfilled entirely: the desire to see my family's town in Karalia, now occupied by Russia and difficult to enter. To visit a country of origin is to lay down expectations and see how they line up with reality, a puzzle that comes together no matter how you piece it.

The moose continued
spindle legs and
antlers eaten
by darkness
and gone.

In my own journey across the road, the destination was not herring or cross-country skiing. It had nothing to do with Finnish goth rock or the national sport of wife-carrying or being named after a bedpan. I realized it was never about getting to a physical place. It was about accessing a space in my mind that allowed for my present-day family in Finland to coexist with the nostalgia of my past.

These days, I'm spending less time spelling out my name for baristas and more time dreaming up the vacation where I'll introduce my own children to the country of their heritage. I wonder what space Finland will occupy for them, and if they'll recognize the moose when they see him, through the curling birch trees, under the violet sky at midnight.

Tarja Parssinen is a writer, performer, and cofounder of Moxie Road Productions, which organizes literary events and helps women market and publish their own work. Her writing has appeared in the *Washington Post*, *Salon*, and *The Huffington Post*. Tarja lives north of San Francisco with her husband and two boys.

Flares

Lisa Witz

That night, I was nestled with my five sisters on the twin bed in the middle room while my three brothers roamed our five-bedroom home. I don't remember who was the keeper of that room at that time—it rotated over the years—but I do remember that I was seven years old and my parents were away, on an anniversary trip to Hawaii, and that I missed my mom desperately. She had recently had a mastectomy and radiation, but the doctor cleared her for the trip. I felt like I had almost lost her and now she was gone, thousands of miles away.

I lay on the twin bed that wasn't mine, listening to the music my sisters were blasting on their cassette player. Carole King's voice serenaded us as she sang "You've Got a Friend," and I wanted to call out my mother's name and have her come running. I took Carole King literally, and whispered Mom's name and waited, hoping somehow she'd magically return from her trip. I wanted her to hold me. I wanted her to be in her bedroom down the hall from mine, not halfway across the Pacific Ocean.

Just then, outside the window, bright flames in the sky dropped down toward earth and dissipated into the night. The sky was so black—not dusk, not moonlight, but pure ebony—and I can still see the bright yellow-orange flames bursting through the night, slower than fireworks but faster than hot air balloons, first shooting down toward the ground and then halting, as if a parachute had been released to ensure a graceful landing.

"What are they?" I asked.

"Maybe the Coast Guard, or maybe something else, I don't know," one of my sisters replied.

The flames were far off in the distance, but they still sent shivers up my spine because they were so foreign, nothing we had ever seen before. I only dared look because my sisters were with me—as if somehow, if there were an attack on our home, on our farm, on our country, they could protect me. I was afraid of violence and of conflict—the sight of men physically fighting still scares me—but with my sisters' protective arms around me in bed, I knew I'd be safe that night.

Five years passed, and I was on the brink of becoming a teenager. After Hawaii, my mother had slowly withered away, cancer cells filling her body. My bedroom was next to the middle room then, which had remained unoccupied after the last sister went off to college. They had all moved on—marriages, careers, travels—and I was the only sister left at home. My father took care of me as best as he could, but he didn't know how to cultivate the workings inside the house. He was a man of the outdoors, managing our thousand acres of sheep and cattle. My brothers and my father fought: over how to raise the animals, over how to spend our income, and eventually over ownership of our land. One time, in the kitchen, I saw my brother push my father up against the wall, his hands a noose around my father's neck, redness turning to blue in his face. I crouched in the corner next to the pasta colander and covered my eyes, though I could still see through the slits of my fingers.

Later, after that fight in the kitchen, I went into the middle room and lay on the bed that wasn't mine and dreamt of my sisters, of my mother, and of that night we saw the fires in the sky while Carole King's voice echoed in the bedroom.

The flares remain a mystery. They may have been paratroopers from the nearby Coast Guard base practicing landing in the night skies. To fight the communists? To fight in Afghanistan or Iran or some other war that took place in the early eighties? I don't know. But I do know the flares represented power and fear, two dominating themes from my patriarchal, Italian Catholic childhood.

Where Dad was the powerful one in our family—he carried the purse strings, and his deep voice bellowed us into line—my mother was quiet, submissive. When she did speak, her words carried tremendous weight. She told all of us to get out—to go to college, get an education, travel the world. Even on her deathbed, she told us to continue pursuing our dreams. Her parenting style worked: nine children, all college graduates.

My sisters finished my mother's work after she died: one took me to Japan, another continuously wired me money while I was in Spain, others threw going-away parties as I went from adventure to adventure. One housed me for years. Twenty-dollar bills in an envelope. Sunscreen. Fresh clothes. A waitressing job. Their strength pushed me to see outside the lines of our childhood, beyond the fences bordering our property.

I often think about that seven-year-old girl lying on the bed, cocooned by her older sisters, and I wonder what would have happened if she hadn't gotten out, if she had never made it to college or traveled the world or opened her eyes to see past the fences of her family farm. If she had stayed in the bedroom, watching the golden flares at night, hating the communists, and obeying the rules of her family's religion, adhering to the patriarchal dynamic. If she had continued to stay silent and pray each Sunday after confession and turned her eyes when her older brother, now a man, beat her father until his face was crimson red. I wonder about the path she didn't take and how she was able to slip out from under the power and fear; or if, like most things from her childhood, it still does reside deep down in her soul.

———

In the mornings, my youngest child slips his lean little body into bed next to me. He's stealthy and doesn't murmur a whisper as he finds the perfect spot to fit his body against mine and radiate warmth. I crave this moment, this time for us to connect before the activities of the day begin, this moment where we cocoon, and I realize I am the veil of protection for this little boy. I am the protector now—the keeper, the nurturer, and the cultivator—and I take all of my wisdom from the mother I lost and the sisters who raised the little girl watching the bright flares in the dark of night.

Lisa Witz grew up the youngest of nine children on a sprawling cattle and sheep farm north of San Francisco. She left the small town to feed her wanderlust, living in Japan, Spain, and the Pacific Northwest. She now lives near San Diego with her husband and three children, and they often visit the farm to hike the trails of her childhood. Her writing has appeared in *Brevity*, *Literary Mama*, *Feminine Collective*, *Mamalode*, *Mothers Always Write*, and, daily, at the kitchen table.

The Trunk

Veronica P. Derrick

I purchased the trunk for my then two-year-old son through a catalog called *Wisteria*. It's a small miracle that I still remember the name, eighteen years later, when just last night I lay in bed unable to remember the name of our friend's daughter, the one who skied with the girls every weekend this past winter. I particularly liked the catalog because of the cheeky descriptions they used to sell their products, and how they listed two customer service phone numbers: one for John, who took compliments, and one for Sue, who took complaints.

Constructed out of wood and protected by a rattan covering, the trunk was advertised as an antique Chinese suitcase. The thought of stowing Grant's childhood memories inside its sturdy frame struck a chord deep in my new-mother psyche. I pictured it traveling with him when he left home as a tall, bronzed young man ready to see the world.

It's ludicrous the things you imagine with your first child.

Take, for example, the bright red model biplane constructed from metal and wire that I purchased for his first birthday. I envisioned it hanging over his bed like a type of guardian angel.

It would only be taken down occasionally, and under my careful supervision. I was sure that one day far in the future, Grant would bring his children to visit me, and, at their insistence, he would pull the plane down and they would play with it together. It's still floating around in a box somewhere below the house, but the drag wires were broken before I managed to get it hung. By the time his fifth birthday rolled around, the wings were loose and it was missing a wheel.

The trunk, though—the trunk lived up to expectations. The thick metal latches withstood his small, overeager hands opening and closing them to put in or take out treasures. The hinges, already over a hundred years old when I purchased the trunk, still open today without complaint, even though Grant's hoard grew to the point where he had to sit on the lid to get the latches closed.

Like *The Giving Tree*, the trunk was stalwart when asked to go above and beyond its designated duties, serving as Grant's nightstand for several years. In that new role, the trunk endured the slap of his hand every morning as he silenced the alarm clock, and it carefully balanced sugary drinks stealthily snuck upstairs. The trunk was also the place where Grant rested the remote for his bedroom light every night before drifting off to sleep. Afraid of the dark, he preferred to leave the light on until he was safely in bed, under his covers.

Grant's nest egg of childhood memories must weigh over fifty pounds. His baby rattle is inside, the silver one in the shape of a moon that his uncle Tom purchased at Tiffany's. Thomas is there too, along with Woody, Buzz, and Jessie.

An A+ is emblazoned across his kindergarten ABC book even though his O's look more like the yawning mouths of ghosts than an actual letter from the alphabet. One entry in his second-grade Daily Language Book reads, "Dear Justin. I like Pokumon <u>very</u> much to! I have been playing Pokumon Llef green a lot. Wut is your favrit Pokumon?" A note from the teacher on the bottom of the page gently reminds him, "No more writing about Yu-Gi-Oh or Pokemon."

A poem from his sixth-grade writing portfolio makes me laugh.

If I were in charge of the world
Id cancel; High School Musical
The war in Iraq
Alarm clocks
And Miley Sirus . . .

I mist up looking at a note he left for me in seventh grade. In giant letters, "GOOD NIGHT MOM!!!" A pair of lips is hastily drawn underneath, and next to the lips, "(kiss here I did)."

There's the Christmas card decorated with holly leaves that he received in eighth grade from Maranda, the first girl he ever kissed. His ninth grade class schedule still has his locker combination, 3-17-07, attached.

Some things I added afterwards. His three Game Boys. His high school water polo cap. His well-worn leather wallet with forty-seven dollars inside.

I thought one day he'd get a kick out of rummaging through the trunk, puzzling over things he didn't remember and cherishing those that he did. Mostly I thought that whenever Grant opened it up, he'd be reminded of how much I love him.

Some of the items in the trunk were never supposed to be there. The lock of his beautiful golden hair with a note from Forest Lawn stapled to the ugly, dark-blue bag that reads, "This lock of hair includes roots for DNA/testing purposes." Or the program for his memorial service with his beaming fourteen-year-old face splashed across the front. Desecrations that the trunk shouldn't have to bear, but I didn't know where else to put them.

A year after Grant died, we moved to Northern California, taking the trunk with us. Today, it sits on the floor outside our guest room. When I pass it on the way to my office, I look away. I know it's only wood and glue, but I can't shake the feeling that the trunk is still waiting expectantly. I don't know how to tell it that the journey it's been prepping for all these years has been inexplicably canceled.

Veronica P. Derrick is a renewable energy lawyer, writer, and Girl Scout leader. She's currently working on a teen fantasy novel and a memoir. She lives in Mill Valley, California, with her family.

Ghost

Thais Nye Derich

I am lying in bed resting, while my two boys build a pillow fort in the next room, when I feel it. A weight like a heavy blanket pressing on my body. Instantly, I know there's a ghost in the room. My eyes pop open. The familiar warmth of a presence envelops me; it's like stepping off a small, air-conditioned hopper plane onto a Hawaiian tarmac, directly into thick, hot tropical weather.

I can tell when there are multiple dead people in a room or just one. I can tell if they're standing still or walking around. I can feel them get closer and move farther away. This time, it's just one and it's in the corner. I sit up and cross my legs. "Deanna?" I ask. It's my birth mother.

⁓

Our previous house in San Francisco, where we lived for seven years, and where my two kids were born, was built on top of a former graveyard. The University of San Francisco resides on it too. Eighty-seven years ago, the city dug up all those dead people and moved them to a new graveyard south of San Francisco. Then they built the university and homes, *our home*, over the top of the old graves. One time we found a headstone in the garden.

I felt ghosts for the first time in that house. To keep them from touching me while I slept, I set a metaphysical boundary. "This is my space," I'd say aloud to the ghosts each night. "Do not cross this perimeter."

It worked. But it wasn't until we moved out to the suburbs and into this new home, not built on a graveyard, that the ghosts stopped coming. I was relieved. The air felt lighter, less humid and heavy. Until today.

Deanna disappeared from my life when I was four years old. Not dead. Just gone. My brother, sister, and I grew up with our dad and his wife, the woman who raised me and who is my mom. But we spent summers in Arizona with Deanna's mother, my grandmother, who made us homemade lemon squares and cut up fresh grapefruit from her tree in the backyard. When Grandmother was ninety-two and ailing, her only choice was to move in with Deanna in Florida.

While visiting Grandmother before she died, I saw Deanna for the first time since she'd left us. That visit was strained. She gave me a tour of the bars where she hung out during the years I was growing up 2,400 miles away. Why did she think it was important to show her grown daughter where her dog would sit outside the local dive bar so that he could still see her in there drinking?

After my grandmother passed, Deanna's mental stability deteriorated further. She thought someone was walking into her apartment, changing the time on the clock, moving her wallet, and stealing her keys. She'd yell, "Help! Help!" off her balcony or down the hallway in her condo complex. The groundskeeper told me he found her in the electrical closet one day, just standing there looking totally confused.

She offered me rye crackers and liverwurst. She ate a Reuben fish sandwich that she'd left in her car in the hot Florida sun because she didn't believe in refrigeration. "Oh honey, I just go to Subway once a week and buy five sandwiches. Then I eat one a day at around noon." She pulled out a half-full glass from the fridge and topped it off with more vodka.

It was clear Deanna suffered from addiction and mental illness. I kept my distance and put my ghost barrier up, even though she was neither dead nor a ghost. Seeing her with my own eyes and hearing her distorted logic made me feel better about her abandoning us. We were better off without her. Still, I harbored a childish fantasy that she'd always wanted us back.

Instead, she told me, "Leaving you three kids was the best decision that I ever made."

I didn't blink. My Adam's apple bulged as I swallowed in my dry throat.

Back home in California, I hugged my children and husband. Several weeks later the Florida police called my cell phone. The landlord wanted her out, the neighbors wanted her gone, and the police told her, "If you keep calling us about nonexistent intruders, you're the one we're going to put in jail."

Now that people knew Deanna had a capable family member, my phone rang multiple times a day. I scrambled to find her a new apartment. The court granted me power of attorney. Her doctor helped me get her a psychological evaluation.

What started as a simple one-off visit to my grandmother became a twenty-hour-a-week job. Why was I helping her? Because she could end up on the street. Because I had learned—through raising my own children—that being pregnant, birthing, and taking care of kids from zero to four isn't nothing. Because helping her was how I could honor what she had done for me, even with all her flaws.

My sister and I started planning to move Deanna closer so we could become care-providers to a mother who had abandoned us. A mother who had no money. A mother with an escalating health crisis. We thought we could figure something out.

But before we could move her, she developed an infection in her gut, couldn't eat, and went in for a feeding tube. She told the doctor that she didn't want to live that way, but there was no choice—she wasn't expected to live longer than two weeks without it. And then another call came—she'd had a heart attack. "Ten people are in there trying to revive her. But I'm not sure that she wants this. Should I tell them to stop?" the doctor asked. "You're her power of attorney."

I gave the "do not resuscitate" consent to the doctor. But who was I to end Deanna's life? I didn't really know her. Should I have had them resuscitate her? Forced her to accept the feeding tube?

And now, two weeks after her death, Deanna is here. Perhaps she has come to say good-bye.

My bedroom is thick with humid air. My ghost shield is up. I hear my kids, who are deconstructing the couch into a three-bedroom home, on the other side of the wall. They never met Deanna, and I didn't refer to her as their grandmother, only as my birth mom, even though a piece of her lives in them.

Deanna keeps her distance up in the corner near the books. She doesn't speak. But I'm not afraid of asking questions when the answers may be uncomfortable. I draw in a big deep breath to calm my nerves.

"Are you upset?" I ask.

Is she mad that I didn't have the doctors resuscitate her? No heat builds in the room. Her ghost remains neutral, like her visit isn't about how she died. She came to see me on her way out, perhaps? Is this the apology I used to crave? Is she trying to make peace?

I prop up some pillows and lean back to show that I'm ready for a conversation. I still want more from her, even now when she's dead. To muffle the noise of my rapidly beating heart, I cover it with both hands. I don't want to project my thoughts onto what she might be trying to tell me from up there in the corner. I breathe and sit. I want her to really see me. The dust particles in the corner swirl. The sideways afternoon light shines in on the bookcase.

After my initial shock about her death, relief rushed in. I could end my search for a medical nurse to fly with her across the country and for the right place for her to live. I no longer needed to fear having her close to me. Did she die so suddenly as a favor to us? "Thank you," I decide to say, aloud.

A thump on the floor tells me that my boys are probably standing on their heads on the couch and falling off. I need to get back to them. Deanna's ghost keeps her distance in the corner. I don't want her to go. I want her to love me.

"Ouch!" I hear from the other side of the wall. She never met her grandchildren. Maybe she'll peek at them in the other room? I get out of bed.

The dust particles move quickly.

With my hand on the door knob, I look up one last time. She had given me what she had the capacity to give.

The sunlight fades, the dust slows until it settles on the shelf. The air thins like fog burning off the coast. She's always been gone, but now she's really gone. I smile and then turn away, suddenly grateful for my ability to feel ghosts.

As I open the door, the children shriek with joy. I try to wiggle my adult body into the various rooms of the pillow fort, but only my head can fit. They giggle and worm through the tunnels without toppling a single wall. They pop out the other end, and I swallow them up in my arms.

Thais Nye Derich is the author of *Second Chance: A Mother's Quest For a Natural Birth After a Cesarean,* a Foreword INDIES Book of the Year Finalist. Her writing has appeared in national and international online and print news outlets, blogs, radio, podcasts, and literary magazines. When she's not working on her second book, Thais is touring the country speaking and coaching with her Write Your Impact book program.

ROOTS

Scales

Cynthia Lehew-Nehrbass

My daughter teeters on the edge of the flat platform, trying to stretch up tall, right shoulder lifted from holding ballerina Froggy tight beneath her armpit.

"Ninety-three point four pounds," the nurse at our family clinic announces and scribbles on her clipboard. My petite twenty-two-year-old with Down syndrome and hearing loss has been losing weight for months despite constant efforts to feed her, chewing reminders, and favorite treats.

"She's maintaining," the nurse adds, and I exhale. Sarah steps off the scale and the red numbers zero out. Small success.

~~~~~~~~

When I was three, I used to stand on our clunky bathroom scale, mesmerized by its *clink* and *ching* as the dial searched for a number. If I wiggled my toes, it would shift left or right; if I jumped on quickly, I could force the red line to the biggest number and cause it to stick. On and off, on and off, I tried to see how fast I could make the metal gauge spin.

My friends' bathrooms also had this toy, in various colors and shapes; even Pops' farmhouse had one on the green lino- leum floor under the shelf that held his Old Spice cologne, and Grandma's was hidden in her hallway closet under piles of linens. For years, I kept secret the allure of the scale's play with numbers and my equal fascination with why, when my mom climbed it in her moo-moo robe, she'd either smile or frown at the number revealed near her toes. A number that had the power to dictate her mood, the clothes she'd choose, and how much food she'd eat that day. Worth-in-numbers.

Wall-to-wall windows chill the gastroenterologist's office. Down the hall, my husband puts our daughter on a glass-topped scale while I fill out her lengthy medical forms, family history, and the results of the swallow study that videoed her lack of chewing and the gagging up of barium-layered crackers. Jeff's voice booms an enthusiastic, "Way to go, high-five!"

I'm hopeful for a weight gain, despite Sarah's baggy floral leggings, but when they enter the room, he announces, "Ninety-two." She's lost yet another pound.

I mentally prepare a protein-dense smoothie and batch of chocolate chip cookies for her when we get home.

During the first months of her life, Sarah was weighed at home weekly in a portable fabric sling that hung from a pulley, hook, and dial. Because of a massive hole in her heart and failure to thrive in utero, she was born early and weighed less than three pounds. Too weak to nurse, I gave her doll-sized bottles of vitamin-fortified formula. I'd wake her every few hours to feed her slowly, so as to not tax her heart, making sure she didn't turn mottled or blue.

160

By her six-month birthday, she'd reached ten pounds on the cardiologist's steel cradle scale, her chest finally big enough for open-heart surgery. The task of growing Sarah, my first job requirement of motherhood, accomplished.

One summer evening when I was in fifth grade, my Kansas cousins thought it would be fun to bring Pops' scale out to the cracked sidewalk just south of the old brick barbecue. We placed it near the ice cream maker that was churning Grandma's peaches and cream recipe, and then took turns watching the rock salt and ice scoot the perimeter of the barrel while comparing our numbers on the scale.

Months earlier, in math class, we'd converted our weights from kilograms to pounds. My 45 kilograms, heavier than most of the girls, was multiplied by 2.2046226218 and landed at just over 99 pounds. I wondered how many bowls of deliciousness it would take to finally reach the triple digits. I knew it would happen someday; my pediatrician had predicted that I would eventually weigh 135 pounds. But I wasn't ready yet. So while I watched everyone devour their cold and creamy treat, I pushed mine around until it melted into sugary milk, then poured it down the sink, leaving only the soft sweetness of low-calorie peaches.

In my third childhood home, the old scale ended up in the basement next to the modern stall shower. We had a fancier one in the upstairs bath, but I preferred the one most certain not to betray me. My mom had a habit of asking me how much I weighed whenever she'd see me hovering near the scale. I thought it was merely motherly interest, until one day near the end of ninth grade. "We weigh the same," she elated after my reveal, and then grinned her way down the hall to the laundry. It wasn't the smile she used when I played the piano for her friends, but more like the beaming expression when I officially became a woman, as if I'd entered some special mother-daughter sorority.

I was devastated. I wanted to be like her, a dedicated teacher and mom, but I didn't want to share the same burden of weight that might someday cause me to call myself fat, compare my friends' sizes, or obsess over losing weight before visiting Grandma each summer.

As the gastroenterologist examines Sarah, she asks a bunch of questions and suggests we schedule some labs and procedures, see a nutritionist, and weigh Sarah once a week at home. When I reveal we don't own a scale, the doctor says, "Go buy one." What a loaded request; she has no idea. I abandoned scales years ago, casting my gaze away at the doctor's office, walking past them at the gym. "Do you want to know your weight?" the nurses still ask. "I don't do that anymore," I say.

Down the narrow hall from my college ballet studio towered my nemesis, an eight-foot-high antique scale. Its metal frame skimmed the low ceiling and its broad base, nearly a foot off the floor, waited for me every morning after class. The circus-size round head, with its palm-wide numbers, taunted me. The platform was so bulky I had to consciously step around it and try to withstand its magnetized pull. On those days of success, I'd feel a twinge of empowerment, a small glimmer of hope that I could defeat this beast that determined my self-worth as a dancer and whether I would eat or purge. But more often than not, I'd climb the monster, watch it quickly grab a number and flash my day's fate in front of me. No therapist, no reasoning roommate, no fainting spell or heart palpitation could match the power of that scale. My only choice was to exit class from the other door, walk the other way, and disappear.

My beautiful seventy-four-year-old mom climbs onto her doctor's scale and pushes a celebratory fist into the air. "Yes! Five pounds!" All chronic ailments and symptoms put aside, her lifelong goal to be a smaller version of herself—that teenager who needed to fit into her parents' clothing store samples—still trumps everything else in her world.

From across the room, I witness the woman I've wanted to emulate rejoice on top of her "worth-finder" and I wonder if this trapping we share will reclaim me when my strength to resist and my hard-learned body acceptance gives way to the aging of my bones and sinew.

The nutritionist's office is intimate and low lit, with two comfy leather chairs in the corner and a basket of smiley-faced bouncy balls on the table. Sarah settles into a chair and picks up an orange ball, oblivious to her upcoming hospital visits: four hours of dental extractions and restorations, planned because of tooth decay from pocketing food and night grinding; an endoscopy to biopsy her stomach and dilate a narrowed esophagus; and a separate surgery to deal with a sick tonsil. I hold all this for her. All Sarah knows is that she gets to play on a new scale, mesmerized by its red LED light, much like I was once by the *ching* of a dial.

"Chocolate every day," the nutritionist advises, and Sarah signs a circled "C" on the back of her hand with a huge smile. Chocolate—her favorite word next to happy and friend.

After a week of incredible amounts of goodies, protein and fat, and marathon sessions of eating, Sarah is up a pound. "You are doing a great job," the nutritionist offers me, and for that moment I accept the compliment. From our conversations she's aware of my decades-long struggles with weight and eating. But this time I'm doing it right. Yes, I may be my mother's daughter, carrying burdens of scales past, but I have learned the most from being my daughter's mother. I catch Sarah's grinning ball and toss it right back.

That night, Sarah dances naked in front of the mirror after the bath that washed dinner's mess from her hair. There is plenty of room on the cool white ceramic to dance, but no room for any scale. Her narrow chest has a huge scar over her heart that stretches long as she lifts her arms to twirl like ballerina Froggy. My daughter is larger than life in her tiny body, perfect in all her imperfections. She stops and giggles. Her hand caresses her face, signing "beautiful"—first to herself, then to me.

Cynthia Lehew-Nehrbass holds a BS in Dance and a Certificate in Creative Nonfiction from the Loft Literary Center in Minneapolis. Her writing appears in the anthologies *Windows into Heaven* and *Mamas Write*, the National Down Syndrome Congress Newsletter, and other publications. She's also a dance teacher, a certified health coach, and a volunteer parent advocate for families who have children with special needs.

The Burden of Silence

Sweta Chawla

Family History:
Diabetes—check
High Blood Pressure—check
Arthritis—check

I imagine very similar ticks on the questionnaires of the other South Asians who have sat in yellow-walled, no-windowed, very small doctor's offices like this one, filling out tedious family medical history forms, just as I have a hundred times before. Indians have high rates of diabetes and heart disease, and this is something they are not ashamed to share. You would know this if you were a fly on the wall at any Indian family's home on Diwali, Christmas, or Auntie and Uncle's twenty-fifth jubilee.

"Is there salt in this dish? You know I have high blood pressure."

"You should drink karela juice . . . it's very good for bringing down glucose."

"Beta, can you bring some extra diabetes test strips from the pharmacy?"

But on this particular form, there is an extra box to check. One I have never ticked before, never even noticed in all the times I've had to divulge our family history: *Nervous Breakdown: Mother—check.*

I wonder if any of the other South Asians have noticed this box?

My earliest memory of snapping my mother back to present reality was when I was eight. I was sitting on one of our brown metal immigrant dining room chairs in Union City, New Jersey, in my bright blue My Little Pony nightdress, licking my fingers after scooping up my very favorite Indian sabzi, *aloo gobi*, with a piece of chapati, then dipping it in yogurt and racing it into my mouth. All while making sure not to skip a beat of *Inspector Gadget* as my mom "broomed" the floor.

Ten minutes into dinner, it started. The yelling—but at whom, I don't know. It was in Sindhi, my family's indigenous tongue, and only one of us in the room spoke that language.

Did she know I was in the room? Did she care? Did I care? Or was I only concerned that I couldn't hear what Penny was saying to her uncle on TV?

I don't know if I ever questioned what was happening to my mom in these moments. She would turn her head, widen her eyes, clamp her teeth, and look like she was fighting with an imaginary person. I don't know if it just became normal, a reflex, to go up to the woman who birthed me and literally snap her out of it. If I was close enough, I would nudge her on the shoulder, the way a buddy would do to a friend. If she was too far away and I was too lazy to bring her back physically, I would just yell, "Stop!" Most times, this did the trick.

My role for the next two decades was to snap her out of it, to bring her back to reality—even on her deathbed in a hospital in Mumbai. Sometimes I wonder if my brother and father even knew or noticed. To this day, we have never uttered a word about it.

It was only when I had a family of my own that I started to really care about why she did this. Maybe I was afraid of inheriting it. I did not want my children to bear the pain of my own upbringing.

Who was she? Why did this happen? I wanted to know.

In many ways, my mom was larger than life. She could work a room like no tomorrow and had a laugh that roared louder than a lion. Growing up in India, she was the smartest of eight children and had big dreams of becoming a doctor. Instead, she was required to enter into an arranged marriage to a man who at the time had little education.

Despite her fate, she had a tenacity and faith that gave her tremendous strength. When I was just two years old, my mother, brother, and I joined my father in the United States. Unlike many Indian wives, my mom refused to be subservient. She wanted to work—a bold desire, at that time, in a foreign country. Her chemistry degree didn't get her far, but she was determined to have her independence, so she took a job in a factory. For twenty years she woke up at five o'clock in the morning and with the utmost gratitude she showed up and did her job. She didn't even have a driver's license.

She was also a stingy "Guju" who made me wear my brother's hand-me-down sneakers, even on picture day. But when it came to moving us out of a cockroach-infested apartment and into a nice neighborhood during my impressionable teenage years, it was she who slapped down the twenty-five grand so we could finally have our own rooms. It was she who helped pay my tuition to pharmacy school. On the outside she was strong, independent, social, a woman of devout faith.

It wasn't until I became pregnant with my own child that I wanted to know more.

"Auntie, did my mom breastfeed me?"

"What were her pregnancies like?"

Her replies were unsatisfying. "I don't know, Beta, I don't remember," she would say. One unanswered question after another.

But I didn't give up. When my son was fifteen months old, we took the fourteen-hour flight to India. I was determined to get some answers.

Even Nani, who wasn't my real grandmother but was like a mother to my mother, had no answers for me. Sitting on a wooden bench on a hill an hour away from Bombay, over the sweetest fresh strawberry ice cream, I finally asked. "Nani, what happened to Mummy?"

"Well she and your papa moved to Calcutta and she went into shock. When she came back the doctor said she had schizophrenia."

Schizophrenia? "Umm . . . impossible, Nani!" I managed her medicines, and she didn't take anything for her brain. There is no way she would have not deteriorated more after so many years without treatment.

"I don't know, Beta."

I gave up. I stopped asking questions. But then my cousin's mother finally gave me something to work with.

"Calcutta was a very violent place in the '60s," she told me. "Your mom saw something very bad happen and went into shock."

Even though she gave me no details and skirted around the pain like we Indians do, there was a part of me that knew my mom didn't just see something. Something had happened to her. I will never know for sure, but my heart tells me she was physically hurt and that trauma lived in her body and mind like a prisoner in solitary confinement.

"Your father didn't know what to with her, so he brought her back to Bombay," she said, "but she refused to live with your grandmother."

There were no cushy couches and shrinks in India at that time. There was no post-traumatic counseling.

I asked one of my aunts, "Why do Indian people hide certain problems and never ask for help?"

My sister-in-law looked at me with wide eyes. *I can't believe you just asked that.* We both knew the rules: heart and sugar problems were acceptable, but having, or even talking about, mental illness or something that could really take you out, like cancer, were no-nos. But, I didn't care about these rules anymore.

My aunt looked at me and said, without batting an eyelash, "Because people gossip."

I can't help but wonder if my mom is looking down at me, thinking, *Sharam, do you not care about your family name? You never knew how to keep your mouth shut.* Or would she understand that even though her suffering was hidden, it deeply affected my identity and choices. Would she understand how her pain rippled through me as I decided to become a doctor of pharmacy to fulfill her dream of being a doctor, hoping that I could heal her? My own way of coping after spending my childhood watching our matriarch suffer.

Or would she understand that I am making the choices I wish she could have made. And that I am breaking the wounding patterns of my lineage through talking instead of staying silent.

Sweta Chawla is a retired professor of pharmacy turned blogger and life/soul coach. When she is not writing, she is salsa dancing, Bollywood jamming, or traveling, with her family or alone.

Rubicon

Emily Myers

The rental apartment in San Francisco was sparse. Spring sunshine bleached the walls, and the gray linoleum was warm under my bare feet. My newborn was asleep in my arms, and I had the phone wedged between my shoulder and jaw. I missed my mum and I told her so.

"I miss you too," she replied, and the phone crackled as it always did when she moved away from the window.

The line between us stretched from blistering California to damp, rural England. Interference was expected. I pictured her in the squat stone cottage at the cove, with its granite walls and small square windows. She'd be in the room she called "The Snug," with its view of the road and the stream beyond, cutting its way through the narrow valley. Trout would be swaying their tails slowly in the whiskey-colored water. Then, suddenly, they would be gone. Bamboos and outsized, waxy camellia bushes bordered the stream as it coursed alongside the road, switching back and forth another half mile before spilling out into the sea. I could hear my mother moving, the whisper of her polyester vest as she sat down. I imagined her in those dark green wingback chairs, facing the granite mantel and the fire. Dad would be out with the dogs. There'd be logs burning in the grate, spitting and popping.

"I wish you were still here. If only you were here, I could nip over and help you." She sounded baffled.

"I know," I said. Her sweet celery soup came into my mind and with it, the smell of sweated onions.

"What are you doing over there?" she said. I imagined her gently shaking her head. It wasn't a question, just an expression of what was missing.

I swayed, looking down at Max, three weeks old, his lips blistered from nursing. My whole body ached. "Dom got a job, remember?" I said, a sad laugh in my throat. I did not answer the question she was really asking, which was why I had agreed to the move.

I wanted to say it felt like I was standing alone in the middle of a rainstorm. I could see the water making rivulets all around me, my feet in the mud. The water was moving with such speed, and yet surrounded by this torrent of rain, it felt like nothing would ever change. I would always be here, watching this kind of water, on this kind of riverbank. What I wanted to say was that I missed the geography of my childhood, its familiarity, and that a nostalgia had crept in uninvited and was sitting heavily on my chest.

My mother told me about gossip in the valley. There was a dispute about who should get the firewood from a fallen tree. Dad and Francis were going head to head with their camellias in the Penzance flower show. Eamon was back in hospital and "Penny and Co" (she meant Penny and her three grown daughters) were up at The Nook with Val, who was now bedridden. "You know how tight that family is," she said.

I waited for my personal rainstorm to pass, slowly piecing together the jigsaw of my child, pulling genes from here and there—the dimples, the turn of his mouth and the curve of his nose—trying to make sense of things, looking for clues about who he might become. The tangle of geography and destiny turned over in my mind like a knot I was trying to undo.

"It feels like you've been away thirty years," said my mother during one of our long-distance calls.

"A lot has happened," I said.

I wanted to say that I was beginning to understand the enormity of motherhood, that my love for my child felt like a giant peony had bloomed in my throat and sometimes it was hard to breathe.

Max's head got heavier. His eyes brightened, and he began to chuckle. He sought me out as we moved about together. Every day the picture of my child, his character, became a little fuller. I knew the eczema on his thumb and the milk spots under his chin. I knew the smell of formula on his breath and how his eyelashes had grown. I knew how he hiccupped when he laughed. He loved his bath, I found out, and I noticed his feet were the length of my thumb. I saw how he pulled his socks off and sucked on them and looked startled when he rolled himself over. He marveled at his hands and gripped my hair when I leaned into his crib. I knew the feeling of his cold fingers and sharp nails on my chest, and how he'd sleep in broad daylight, tolerating the fact that I hadn't put up curtains in his room. I found that the rainstorm had created a river. Familiarity just took time.

My mother came to visit. She came alone because Dad didn't like leaving the cove. There was no one to look after the dogs or the chickens, he said. Mum made it clear she had come to see me, that I was her priority. She meant it with love, but it felt like another kind of suffocation. We stood together in the kitchen. The line between us should have been clear but still it crackled.

"She *is* your mummy," she said to Max, who was, by then, a toddler. "But she is also *my child*." She hugged me awkwardly with one arm. Max ran off, squealing.

⌒

"You're not coming back," she said when she left. Her voice was hollow. We hugged by the front door; a cab was waiting to take her to the airport. She looked exhausted. We were both tired by then. And perhaps she was right. A few months later I was pregnant with my second child.

I have always thought of the cove as the sediment of my being. Something about the permanence of the granite, its rough durability, gray-pink and flecked with quartz. I loved the story of my great-grandmother, Alice Favell, seeing the valley for the first time, scorched with daffodils. She had come from Sheffield with her sickly husband and bought the one-story stone house by the river. Slowly she acquired farmland and outhouses and became something of a proprietress, a plump matriarch with dogs at her heels. The war brought her daughters and a daughter-in-law back into the cupped hands of the cove, where grandchildren ran to the slip and played in the tide pools. A safe haven. Now, men lean on their boats and talk of the past. When Alice died an old woman, she handed the valley to the National Trust to preserve its torpid beauty. Her descendants hang on to what is left. Nothing changes now. No one wants that. It is wonderful and stifling, like another peony blooming in my throat.

⌒

After my mother left, we resumed our weekly phone calls. It was hard for her to find reference points.

"How is that lady we met in the park?" she'd say.

"Oh, I haven't seen her again."

"And the soccer classes?"

"Yes, they've finished."

I'd made a friend with a son Max's age, but to announce it would make me seem sadder and lonelier than I was. I was pulling away, finally coursing my own river. The storm had broken, letting me take big gulps of air. But when I spoke to my mother, I was pulled back to a place that didn't allow for change. We fell back into what we were both missing: each other. In the end, it seemed easier not to call.

My mother had her own interpretation for my silence. "I can't bear to think of you being unhappy," she said.

"I'm not," I said. "I need you to support me." My words felt urgent. "Dom and I are together. We have a healthy child. These are things to celebrate."

What would you prefer? I wanted to say. *Me sleeping on your couch?*

She was slow to reply. "Yes, I get it." She was thinking of her own journey west, decades earlier, how she had left England's heel for its toe when she'd married my dad.

"My mother happily let me go." Her voice was light and filled with a gratitude that seemed to surprise her. Perhaps it was this she had been trying to redress.

Later, she called that moment her "Rubicon," her point of no return. Perhaps it was mine too. In 49 BC Julius Caesar crossed a watershed called The Rubicon and committed himself to a conflict that changed the course of history. I like to think that, for my mother and me, the territory was emotional and put us on a path to peace.

Emily Myers has worked as a radio journalist for the BBC in London. Now living and writing in Brooklyn, she's performed at Listen to Your Mother NYC, and her personal essays have appeared in *Wanderlust Journal*, *Parent Co.*, and *Brain, Child* magazine.

A New Roadmap

Maria Ramos-Chertok

My earliest memory is lying in bed at my grandmother's home, unable to sleep because I was worrying about death. I hadn't yet lost anyone I loved—it was my own mortality plaguing me. Later on, in my early teens, I did a volunteer stint at an old age home. My spirit plummeted as I saw faded lives, nonverbal people with vacant stares, and the feeling of horror— that that could one day be me—never left. I carried it with me for thirty years as the roadmap for where I'd eventually end up.

Until the day I met Ethel Seiderman.

New to Marin County, the mother of two young boys, and, at forty-three, feeling desperate to connect with people I could relate to, I decided to attend a women's forum at a nearby college, figuring it could be a fruitful way to meet like-minded women. The event itself remains foggy in my mind with one exception: toward the end of the afternoon, a five-foot-tall woman with short brown hair, dressed in a style reminiscent of New York fashion icon Iris Apfel, walked up to the microphone. She spoke in a thick accent—saying the word "here" as a two-syllable pronouncement, "he ya." Finally, someone who spoke my dialect, a New Jersey working-class manner of speech that I'd lost after twenty-plus years of living in California.

As much as I loved her language, I gravitated especially to the way her presence defied the stereotypes I held about senior citizens. When this small and powerful woman, who had to be in her seventies, stood at the podium, it felt like the lights had been turned up in the room. I was drawn in like a toddler discovering a firefly. I wanted to learn her secret of aging without seeming old. I tried to introduce myself, but at the end of the event she was swarmed like a rock star by other participants. Yet, on the drive home, I couldn't stop thinking about how much I'd like her to be my friend.

A year later, I was asked to facilitate a meeting for a nonprofit organization working with homeless youth. I was happy to see Ethel's face in the audience, but I knew by then that she was the very-popular-girl-on-the-block, and I'd decided to let my friendship fantasy remain just that.

At the end of the meeting, as I was packing up, she approached me. "Who are you? Why don't I know you?" she demanded.

Flabbergasted, I gave her my name.

"I know your name—I want to know *who you are*!"

I coughed up a few details related to my work as a consultant to nonprofits and added that I'd seen her speak before and had wanted to get to know her ever since.

"Well, what are we waiting for? Let's get together." She dug into her enormous bag to pull out a business card and wrote her cell phone number and her email.

Elated, I held onto her card like it was the neon orange life preserver I needed to stay afloat.

Ethel was ready for a new friendship even in her seventies, and she didn't seem to care about our age difference, approaching me as a contemporary without losing any of the stature that came with her decades of wisdom.

Our friendship took off on the fast and furious track, and we became self-proclaimed soul mates: we both had May birthdays (thirty years and one day apart) and were stubborn Taureans, breakfast was our favorite meal, we believed in writing thank-you cards, we were steadfast in our commitment to social and racial justice, and we loved long walks. Ecstatically, we discovered a mutual fondness for swearing like truck drivers. We'd walk the local trail together out to the Pacific Ocean and whenever I commented on her stamina, she would always reply that her stamina impressed her as much as it did me.

There was also a bond regarding what I'll call religious expansiveness. Like me, she had been born Jewish, which was an important part of her identity, but she was also close friends with a Dominican sister and a Buddhist monk. I admired her ability to see beyond labels and look at one's soul, something I, too, saw as a critical step toward peace.

Three years into our mutual admiration society, Ethel purchased two identical large plexiglass rings embedded with tiny mauve roses. She knew the title of my debut novel was *Rosie's Blues* and that I loved all things roses. She gifted one ring to me and kept one for herself. I announced to my husband that I was officially engaged to Ethel. He forgave my infidelity.

Ethel's social calendar was a sight to behold: meetings on educational equity, the latest art exhibit, community events, sitting on boards, travel to New York and Australia and Bodega Bay to spend time with her family, hanging out with Isabel Allende for dinner, and writing letters to the editor. She was actively involved with a multicultural summer program and hosted meetings in her home to provide mentorship to local leaders working on social justice issues. Ethel showed me again and again that old age didn't have to be sedentary. Engaging in life with passion isn't an age thing—it's a choice, an inner quality.

In the short ten years I knew her, she published two books of personal essays, starred in a film about her life, and received numerous awards. One local college even renamed a program the "Ethel Seiderman Institute for Excellence in Early Education."

Trying to make plans with Ethel required sitting patiently as she studied her paper datebook looking for ways to fit in something else. She always made time for me, even if it meant adjusting another commitment. Her strong value about spending time with people she cared about made me stop and consider who and what I prioritize each day.

So when Ethel invited me to see an exhibit at the San Francisco Museum of Modern Art, I accepted, despite having to put off work commitments for the entire day. We walked down Mission Street toward the museum, and as we passed by Good Vibrations, I encouraged her to come inside, explaining that it was a vibrator store and museum, a once-in-a-lifetime experience. Ethel was game. Several minutes of browsing later, we ended up staring at a large pink vibrator with a long clitoral brush and a big price tag.

A young sales person, a millennial with spiky hair, approached us. "May I answer any questions?"

I had none. Ethel looked at the large contraption on the display table and up at the salesperson. "Why can't you just use your finger?"

I tried to keep from howling with laughter. The salesperson remained composed, nodded her approval, and confirmed that one could certainly use one's finger should that be the stimulant of choice.

Ethel shrugged and, unimpressed by the contraption, walked on.

If I had to choose only one reason to love Ethel forever, that moment in the vibrator store would be it.

Ethel died alone in her home after eighty-four years of life. Her daughter found her lying in bed wearing a Curious George T-shirt with *The New York Times Magazine* open to an article entitled "Occupy Hillary." Hearing about her last days provided me an alternative vision to the tragic deaths of my father, who died in a county mental hospital; my grandmother, who died en route from a hospital to a hospice facility because of hospital billing greed; and my stepmother, who died in an old age home after losing most of her physical abilities. It is always hard for me to imagine their last moments, hoping that they were not scared or lonely or in need of consolation. In contrast, when I think about Ethel, reading in bed and wearing a youthful fashion statement, I don't have the same despair. She left on her own terms, in her own house, in her own bed. I see how this, too, is a gift she has given me. A new image of the last day.

At her memorial service there were hundreds of people, all of whom claimed to be Ethel's best friend. At first it was the communal joke, but then it kind of crept into the crevices of our individual insecurity and each of us, I suspect, either wondered where we actually fell on her list of favorites or secretly believed that we definitively made the top ten. I left her memorial service feeling jealous and wanting to demand a final meeting to certify that she loved me more than the others. I was so beside myself that I went to her grave and spelled out her name in thirteen long-stemmed red roses to prove my love and devotion.

Ethel never stopped expanding the reach of her love, and her life healed a part of me. There was no scarcity model when it came to giving from the heart and giving of herself. She offered me a new roadmap that contrasted with the earlier one I'd held that allowed one to withdraw from life and use age as an excuse not to keep active. Even though she's gone, I now know I have a choice. I can choose to honor every day by awakening to the unknown blueprint of each moment and discard the map that I wrote for myself long before I knew where I wanted to go.

Maria Ramos-Chertok is a writer, workshop leader, and coach who facilitates The Butterfly Series, a writing and creative arts workshop for women who want to explore what's next. She's been a disco queen, law professor, cowgirl, and crisis counselor. She thanks Marin County, California, for being the place where she met Ethel Seiderman.

Back to Havana

Gloria Saltzman

I t's four o'clock in the morning at the Havana International
Airport and my fifteen-year-old daughter, Madeline, and I
are wondering why my mother has not made it through customs
like we have. Finally, a uniformed official comes to let us know
that she is being held back.

"Why?" I ask, trying very hard not to panic.

"Your mother's American passport says she was born in
Havana," he says calmly. But I detect a slightly malicious grin
on his face.

Mom hasn't been back to Cuba since she left with her
family in 1942, when she was seventeen years old. The history
goes like this: My grandparents left Russia for America around
1917, because of the Bolshevik Revolution and the persecution
of the Jews, but weren't able to enter the United States because
of daily immigration quotas. The captain of their boat said
he'd bring them to Cuba instead. "It's very close to Miami," he
assured them. Since swimming over the Atlantic Ocean was not
an option, it took another twenty-five years for my grandparents
to finally reach their intended destination. Mom and her three
siblings were all born in Havana.

"*¡Dios mio!* I bring my daughter and my granddaughter back to my *patria* and this is the welcome I get!" Standing with our own stamped passports, my daughter and I can see and hear my mother. She is fanning herself ferociously and ranting at a young soldier with a pockmarked face and a rifle slung over his shoulder.

We are eventually escorted back to the other side of the customs area, where we find Mom sitting on a straight-backed chair, looking surprisingly relaxed now. My mother is the sort of person who gets very upset over small things, like spilled milk—but when something really serious happens, like being kept at border control in a dictatorship, she seems to go into a trance of calm.

My daughter and I try to conceal our terror as Mom begins talking to the rifle-slinging soldier very familiarly, and all in Spanish. As she converses in her native tongue—as though he is a neighborhood kid—I work hard not to keep my mouth ajar in shock, and I observe her as though she is someone I have never met before.

"So, *mijo*, who do you live with?"

"I live in my mother's house," he answers softly.

"Ah, with your mother, that's what I thought," Mom says with that motherly *I knew it all along* look on her face I know so well. I had seen it every time I finally told the truth after first covering up with a lie.

"Let's go right now to your mother's house. Let's tell her how you treat an old woman when she returns to her *patria*, a woman like your *abuela*. All I want to do is to show my daughter and my granddaughter where I come from. But now you put a bad taste in my mouth for this special return to my own country!"

"Well, *abuela*, how much money do you have with you?" the child soldier asks.

I don't hear what she tells him, but I hear his response: "That is exactly the amount of money you will need to get the correct papers to enter the country and then be allowed to leave again!"

"MOM!" I yell. "Don't answer any more of his questions!" I sense something evil in the way he studies my mother. It reminds me of the way someone looks when they compliment you but really they have nothing but dark or even dangerous thoughts about you.

I glare at him and explain in English, "My mother has been an American citizen for more than sixty-five years."

"Yes, *señora*, I understand that." I imagine a whirl of smoke escaping from his grin and two small red horns beginning to rise up from the back of his head. "But you know, *señora*, once a Cuban, always a Cuban!"

My stomach churns with fear. I honestly don't know if I should take him seriously. We have been cast in a bad movie in a country with armed guards and no sign of an American embassy.

As soon as he leaves her side for a moment, I bend down and whisper in my mother's ear, "Start acting sick, Mom."

My mother rises instantly to her glory. She loves to perform. Incorporating all of the skills she has gathered from reading poetry as a teenager in the *Centro por Judeos*, playing the role of a talking tree in her Yiddish club, and blowing melodiously in her kazoo band, Mom goes into action: "*Dios mio, yo soy diabetica. ¡Me siento enferma!*" Mom fans her face ever more rapidly with her black floral *abanico* that my aunt brought her from Spain, the one she carries with her wherever she goes.

"I think my mother needs a doctor," I say urgently to one of the female border guards who apparently speaks English.

Immediately, a woman wearing a white medical jacket and a stethoscope flung around her neck strides toward us. She seems genuinely concerned about my mother's well-being and speaks to her kindly as she gives her a glass of water. She checks blood pressure on one arm as my mother uses the other to reach for the stack of soda crackers she carries with her in case of nausea. She actually is diabetic, so she also takes a bite of a special candy bar she pulls from her travel bag, exactly for times like this, when she needs a little extra sugar.

Two hours and plenty of bilingual drama later, the customs officials finally let her go. We are told that if we go to a local government office and get the correct visa, there should be no further problem. Within moments, Mom's unspoken gratitude toward me is evident. She breaks into a wide smile and I notice a new, light demeanor about her. It's as though she is growing younger before my eyes.

Miraculously, the hotel van is still waiting for us when we exit the airport into the sultry island air. The driver helps us load our luggage and hoists my mother into the front seat. As the sun rises, we drive along palm-lined roads and fields of sugarcane for the first and only visit my mother will make back to Havana, her homeland.

What could have been a disappointing disaster has instead created a memorable adventure for all of us. My daughter, my mother, and I spend our days and nights exploring Havana. The handsome, dark-haired taxi driver we met outside our hotel is ready for us every morning. He gladly takes us to out-of-the-way places my mother remembers.

Each time Mom explores another setting from her childhood, her cheeks turn a rosy pink to match the wide-brimmed straw hat she wears to protect her pale white skin from sunburn. She cannot stop talking to everyone we meet in her native tongue. Mom is different here. She fits in, in a way I don't think she ever has in the United States. Her family's poverty does not evoke shame in her while we are in Cuba. My parents never had enough money to have a regular cleaning lady. Mom did not go to the hair salon frequently or get her nails done by a manicurist who most likely would have been from a background just like hers. Back in the United States, she often made jabs about the "fancy ladies" in a way that I now understand was envy, even though at the time I interpreted it to mean that they were not as good as she was because of what she was able to live without.

"Oh the fancy ladies go to the opera and get ready for it for days!" she would say with a tone of sarcasm laced with desire.

Here in Havana, Mom is part of a larger whole. Although the political system is not ideal, the citizens are united in their experience of isolation from the rest of the world, and therefore more connected with each other. I see how comfortable she is.

One night we decide to eat at a *paladar*, a home that has been turned into a restaurant and serves authentic Cuban food, an alternative to the state-run businesses. We do not have a reservation, but the owner, a proud gay man, can find a place for us. While we wait, he sits with Mom on a loveseat outside the dining area. He pets her hands and listens as she explains how important it has been for her to be back in Havana. Many times she has told me that homosexuality is against her religion, whatever that means. However, in this instance she is open and tolerant and loving toward this kind man who is holding her heart in his hands as he purrs to her.

I've heard it said that when a person speaks their native language, changes happen. The tone of the voice gets deeper and facial expressions are different. There is a general comfort with oneself that might also transform a personality. It seems to make my mother more accepting and open.

Here in Cuba, speaking her mother tongue, Mom has rediscovered some nearly lost part of herself: her confidence and her own true nature. Maybe that explains why the little ant of a soldier at the airport did not scare her one bit.

Even though I'm grateful that we all took this trip, I now realize I didn't know how much of a risk we were taking: There are more borders to cross than I expected, not just the ones at the airport, but also within my mother's memory and emotional life. In bringing my mother back to her *patria*, I not only see the land she came from, I am also being introduced to a part of her I have only seen glimpses of before—a teenager twirling around in the street like Cinderella at the ball, dressed in her off-the-shoulder, knee-length, black-and-pink floral dress, joyfully singing, "I am just a poor girl from Havana!" She is exuberant as we explore the broken cobblestone streets of her past. And I am happy to dance right alongside her.

Gloria Saltzman is a psychotherapist in private practice in San Francisco. She has an MFA from the University of San Francisco with a focus on poetry and creative nonfiction. She has been published in *The Pharos*, *Tikkun Magazine* online, the *San Francisco Chronicle*, and a literary journal in Paris.

Crossing the Bridge

Marianne Lonsdale

"A re you sitting down?" Mom asked over the phone. "I have to tell you something."

I'd had dinner at my parents' home the previous Sunday and she'd casually mentioned she was seeing a specialist the next day. For months now she'd been having stomach pains and a loss of energy. But my eighty-two-year-old mother was the opposite of the stereotype of seniors whose conversations center on their health. Despite painful arthritis, she still hiked every week on Mount Tamalpais.

"Do you know what kind of specialist you're seeing?" I'd asked.

"Yes, I do," Mom had responded. "The one my doctor told me to see." She'd turned back to the stove. I wasn't sure if she didn't know or just didn't want to tell me.

Now, I sat at my dining table alone, clutching the phone to my ear. My husband and son weren't home yet.

"I have stage 4 cancer," she said, her voice firm and steady. "I have six months to a year left."

I stopped breathing. My forehead felt heavy as her words attempted to penetrate my brain.

187

"Mom, what kind of cancer?" I asked. The news seemed to bounce in an echo chamber as the shock moved through my body.

"I'm not sure. It's everywhere, so the doctor doesn't know where it started. He seemed upset that he didn't figure this out sooner." True to form, she sounded so matter-of-fact.

I remembered her barely touching her plate at a wedding shower last fall. Had I been so self-involved with my family, work, and writing that I'd missed how long she'd been having symptoms?

"So what will the doctors do?" I asked. *What can be done?* I wondered.

"Nothing. And that's okay. I'm glad I don't have to have surgery or chemo. The goal is to keep me comfortable."

I looked to my front door, willing my husband home. I wanted to wrap myself around him.

"I need to leave for a meeting now, so I'm going to hand you to Dad."

Total Mom. Nothing would slow her down. Or force her to go too deep. When Dad got on the line, he couldn't even talk. He choked out a few grunts and hung up the phone.

———

I visited Mom before I left for my writing conference in the Sierras the following Saturday. I'd been slow to call myself a writer. Some friends and most coworkers didn't even know I'd been writing for a decade.

But this year had been a turning point. Along with five other mothers, I'd founded a writing salon. We met monthly to write, talk, and listen to a speaker. Six months after starting, we had forty members. I left our meetings feeling energized and inspired and, with their support, I'd applied and been accepted to a prestigious writing conference in Northern California's Lake Tahoe. I can't say I felt like I'd arrived, but I did feel like I was starting to board the train.

"I'm not sure I should leave for the week," I said as I walked into the house—my childhood home, the one my parents had bought fifty-one years earlier. Mom was sitting on the ratty brown couch in the television room; Dad was next to her, watching the golf channel with the sound muted.

"I still have that novel I wrote before we had kids," Mom said. "It's in a shoebox in the bedroom closet." She'd mentioned her novel years ago, and I'd not asked her any questions about her writing, almost as if I dismissed any ambitions she had besides mother and grandmother.

"Go," Mom said. "Dad's here and your sister's coming by. I'm so happy you're writing."

I perched on the ottoman in front of her chair and held her hand. Even though Mom seemed happy with her choice to stay at home with her kids, she'd always encouraged me to pursue a career and find time for my own interests. I knew she still kept notebooks. A personal journal that she wrote in each morning. And one notebook for each of her grandchildren, where she listed memories.

And now Mom was disappearing. The drugs had dulled her. Her skin had no healthy glow. Yet she gave me her blessing to pursue my writing.

⌒

I visited Mom at least twice a week that summer, making the thirty-mile drive from my home across the Bay Bridge to South San Francisco. Home hospice care started just two weeks after her diagnosis—she was declining quickly, and I wanted to be there as much as I could.

My priorities were clear: Mom, my husband and son, my job and my writing. By a stroke of luck, my writing group had landed a coveted spot at Lit Crawl, a night of literary readings in San Francisco. Over 10,000 people roam the streets, deciding which of about eighty events to attend. I felt like we'd hit the big time by being invited. Most of us were unpublished, and I'm not sure any of us had ever read in front of an audience. I certainly hadn't.

Mom loved the updates on my writing group. Her world was narrowing; she spent most days in the ugly but very comfortable blue faux leather recliner Dad had bought her after her diagnosis. But when I told her our theme for Lit Crawl was "Your Mom Had Sex," she laughed and looked over at my dad.

"I could sure tell stories about that," she chuckled.

"I couldn't keep her off me," Dad chimed in.

Mom wanted all of her family together one last time, so I booked twelve rooms for forty of us at the Best Western in Dixon, a farming community about an hour north of San Francisco. We don't do fancy; a motel with budget rates and free breakfast and coffee met our requirements. Mom and Dad, their eight kids and assorted spouses, girlfriends, one ex-daughter-in-law, fifteen grandkids, and four great-grandkids spent most of that weekend by the pool.

Mom needed a wheelchair to get from her room to poolside and took several naps each day. Sadness flooded my body thinking of how Mom loved to swim and play with her grandkids in pools and lakes. Now she didn't even have the strength to sit at the side and dangle her feet. Only nine weeks had passed since she'd learned she had cancer.

After Dixon, death moved quickly into my childhood home. A hospital bed was set up in the spare bedroom and Dad slept on a twin next to Mom. Two doses of morphine were added to her daily drug regimen. Mom barely spoke and ate only a few bites at meals.

The hospice nurse guessed Mom had two to six weeks left, and suggested that I help Dad make arrangements right away. Lit Crawl was the next week, and I missed the rehearsal. My writing tribe said not to worry—they'd see me at the reading.

Several times a day, Dad stood by Mom's bed and leaned over to hug her. She'd reach up her arms and they'd kiss each other on the lips. "You've always been the one, Anne Marie," he'd say. A smile would fill her face. "You're my girl." It was so touching, so loving, and so painful to watch. When the priest came that week to perform the last rites, he was startled to find Mom and Dad napping together in the hospital bed.

Dad and I made arrangements for the mortuary, the funeral mass, and the reception. I wrote the obituary. And when I could, I escaped to the downstairs laundry room to practice my Lit Crawl piece. I'm a nervous public speaker, and the only way I get through is to go over and over my words so many times that I'm assured muscle memory will take over when I get too anxious.

On the morning of the reading, right before the sun made up its mind to rise, my dad, my sister, and I were at Mom's bedside, holding her hands, waiting for that last belabored breath. I'd been so restrained for weeks, wondering when Mom would die and exactly how her death would transpire. Her body shook, her eyes closed as she pushed out her last breath, and then she lay still. The quiet folded around me like a cashmere stole, and I laid my heart against her body.

I went numb, taking care of details. Men from the mortuary arrived two hours later to transport her body. Dad and I followed to confirm the arrangements. I called the church and emailed the obituary to the newspaper. By noon, everything was arranged and, exhausted, I decided to go home. I'd only been there once that week to grab some clothes. One of my brothers would stay with Dad.

Driving home back across the bridge, trying to fathom that I'd never speak to Mom again, I thought about the irony of my mom dying on the same day as Lit Crawl. I wasn't yet ready to talk to anyone, not even my husband. As soon as I walked in the door I went straight to bed for a nap.

Suddenly, my husband, Michael, was at the bedroom door. "I think you should still read tonight," he said, interrupting my respite.

"It wouldn't be right," I told him, feeling groggy.

"I don't know about any rules on this one," he countered. "You've worked hard to be there. . . ." His voice trailed off. And then he added, "Don't you think your mom would want you to go?"

I took in his words but wasn't ready to make a decision. Later, after my nap, as the warm shower water soothed my body, I realized Michael was right. Perhaps it was unconventional, but my mom would have definitely wanted me to read. She'd encouraged me all along.

Michael drove us back across the bridge to San Francisco that evening. I showed up, sad and yet certain I was where I should be. My friends offered quiet words of comfort and said how glad they were that I'd chosen to be with them.

To attract listeners, we reached out to people passing by, handing out condoms that we'd had scribed with two different slogans: "Writing Is Hard" and "Stroke Your Genius." It worked. Sixty people had crowded into the small space by the time the reading was set to start.

I was first up. My hands didn't shake holding my pages. I read slowly, looking up often into the crowd, feeling in command. But I missed my mom. She'd wanted to be here. My piece, about my son's best friend creating a macramé penis in fifth grade art class, got huge laughs. Mom would have loved the applause that broke out when I finished.

Afterwards, Michael and I sat at an outdoor café and shared wine, salami, a soft creamy cheese, and crusty bread. It was one of those beautiful balmy October evenings in San Francisco. A warm, comforting cloak of sorrow embraced us as I raised a silent toast to my mother for making sure my writing wouldn't hide in a shoebox.

Marianne Lonsdale writes personal essays, fiction, and literary interviews. She's cranking out a novel set in the early 1990s about love and friendship during the AIDS epidemic. Her essays have been published in *Literary Mama*, *Grown and Flown*, and *Pulse*, and have aired on KQED's *Perspectives*.

Angel Maker

Christine I. Peters

"I want to go visit Schleswig-Holstein, just the two of us," my mother announced on the phone last spring. "I'm thinking four days in my hometown. Enough time to discuss all the unspoken things between us."

My stomach plunged at my mother's suggestion. Cooped up together for four days, I could easily capitulate and tell her everything I'd ever kept private. I didn't need her to know whether I was using birth control and I didn't want to divulge the details of my sex life since high school. Yet, I knew she would ask me in ten different inescapable ways until I told her. Assessing other people's psyches, especially mine, had always been my mother's favorite hobby. My little girl dreams revealed penis envy; my dark teen clothing was a symptom of self-hatred. I wished Sigmund Freud could hold my hand.

Come summer, I had firmly resolved to confine topics to above the waistline. I was a grown woman and I was strong now. My mother loathed secrecy, but I would go on this vacation with her to Northern Germany and keep my personal moments confidential.

We drove alongside swaying, mustard-colored rape fields under a cobalt sky that stretched for miles in the level landscape. My mother had grown up in a once-flourishing industrial town that now had the withered charm of an old diva. I hadn't visited in almost twenty years. The familiar aroma of plowed earth made me miss my grandparents, who had lavished me with love whenever I'd called on them—a love they'd withheld from my mother and her siblings.

"Smells moldy, but this black, sandy soil is great for potatoes," my mother said. "We'll eat the best potatoes in the world."

It was afternoon, ample time before dinner. We snuck into the atrium of her erstwhile girls' school, identified the window from which the boys at their lyceum next door had whistled and hooted, and peered through the wrought-iron fence at my grandparent's villa, where a new family with five children now lived. I spotted a rug bar I had dangled on behind the house, and admired how the stream dissected the mossy garden.

"I fed ducks here, like you did when you were little," I said in a joyful rush, thinking we could make this a pleasing memory expedition after all. The river glittered like tiny suns.

"When I was little, I discovered a dead man in the water; he washed up right there," she pointed sternly. "My parents just said I should put it away. They always covered things up, always play-acted to look good."

My hand covered my mouth. "You must have gotten the scare of your life."

"No," she said, more gently and with a faraway expression. "It was Hilda who gave me the scare of my life."

I clung to the concrete balustrade of the bridge, dreading something worse than a corpse. "Hilda, your old housekeeper?"

"Yes, that Hilda. She lived out west in a low-class river hut," my mother said. "It wasn't a rose-covered cottage with a dock back then. The water stank of rotting flesh from the operating tanneries and wool mills. Unemployed men loitered in the streets."

"But you didn't judge her by her background, did you?" I asked.

"I love second chances, but we can't sugarcoat facts. The only good thing young Hilda got from her parents was his red hair and her blue eyes. Hilda was beautiful, with skin like honey-milk. Poor girl started working very young as our maid to escape her circumstances."

A low rumble came from the overcast sky. In my memory, the cobblestone streets were forever glistening with rain. We continued our walk to view the former home of a relative. A gust stirred bits of dirt. I glanced up; clouds were moving in leaden clumps.

My mother pointed out a corner building with a crumbling stone archway. "That's where the angel maker lived."

"Angel maker? What's an angel maker?" It was an abrupt change of topic, but the phrase intrigued me. The notion of people rendering others angelic sounded comical.

"It was hushed up of course, but everybody in this town of frauds knew about the angel maker. Hilda knew. And there are still hidden angel makers in the world," my mother said somberly.

Her words stifled my amusement and now I almost looked over my shoulder to check for descendants of the inquisition or whoever made angels.

My mother held up one palm and consulted her watch. "The best café in town is a five-minute walk."

A short time later, we were drinking spicy coffee in a flagstone courtyard. Crimson blooms spilled from ancient stone troughs. My mother ate my cherry galette, and I picked at the cream torte she hadn't liked.

"The angel maker," my mother said, in the animated way she addressed her high school class, "is a good start for our overdue chat on honesty."

I melted against my backrest. I had expected her to say that she found my life too uncultured, my husband too domineering, my career below potential. Nobody was a hundred percent honest all the time. I glanced at my mother's hand, where her missing wedding ring left a naked white line. Was I supposed to ask about my parents' deteriorating marriage, even if the reasons were intimate? Was I wrong to pretend not wanting children, when for years I had been taking pills, getting injected, and longing for a baby? Was it immoral to deflect painful questions with half-truths?

"Do you think I lie to you?" I asked, keeping a straight face.

She waved impatiently, as if my petty fibs were irrelevant. "The angel maker," she reminded. "Promiscuous men get slapped on the back, women die to protect their reputation. We'll travel back to the fifties to get to this story."

"Sounds more like the Victorian age." I was relieved to get away with listening.

"Hilda worked six days, but Saturdays she did her hair, wore heels, and met her friends at the dancehall. Your grandmother wagged her finger, but I begged for every detail. The music, the dusky ballroom, the handsome boys who bought her drinks. In 1956, there was no pill. Unwed women wouldn't buy condoms at a pharmacy. Men could, but they hated the thick things. Girls stayed strong or faced the angel maker."

"The angel maker hurt girls for falling in love? Or for risking premarital sex? You make it sound like they got murdered!"

"Angel makers could hurt those girls, yes, but that's only part of the truth." My mother's forehead wrinkled in sorrow. "Hilda's sweetheart was an office apprentice with elegant, clean hands. She described how close they danced and how eagerly he kissed her."

"They wanted more than kissing," I said.

"Of course they did. Hilda's parents paid no attention. Her dad was an alcoholic, and people believed her mother was a witch who abandoned her husband to be a dressmaker."

Graphite clouds cast a few first drops of rain. We paid and headed back through the city park. Trees trailed branches in the gushing river, and orange marigolds and stinging nettles freckled the shore.

"I love how green trees look right before a rainstorm," I said.

"They may appear green, but that ground remains poisoned from the cloth mills and leather factories," my mother corrected. "Things aren't what the eye sees. Ever heard of anthrax from animal waste?"

I stared at the innocent-looking soil that held a deadly secret and back at my mother. I slowly nodded. Gullible girls had been in trouble in a place where troubles got glossed over. My childhood had been sheltered in comparison to my mother's and Hilda's. My parents were reliable and kind; the ground I'd played on was safe. I had enjoyed boyfriends without banishment from society, and never relied on men to prevent pregnancy or anything else. So what if my mother dished out guilt and reproach with every phone call. At least she cared enough to ring.

Rain started splattering down, and we ran to shelter under a large oak tree.

"Hilda's mother was the angel maker," my mother said over the splashing drops. "Women visited her seamstress workshop to secretly get abortions. Married women who had one child after the other, or single girls, some no more than children themselves. Hilda's mother used button hooks to position the womb, inserted a section of rubber hose, and pierced the membranes with an awl."

I gasped. "Oh, god, and nothing was sterile, no doctor. What if something went wrong?"

"Women died of bleeding or contamination; it was a well-known risk." My mother sighed. "They were desperate enough to take the chance."

I had read about backroom abortions, and was baffled my mother was acquainted with a person who carried them out. "What about adoption or orphanages?" I asked. "Women's shelters?"

198

"There was adoption, but the orphanages were horrid. Very few places, convents, took pregnant women in until birth. Some unmarried mothers braved the ostracism."

"You said earlier that Hilda scared you to death?" I asked with a sinking feeling.

My mother nodded gravely. "She showed up at our door one day, white as a ghost and shaking all over. Her own mother had given her an illegal abortion and the bleeding wouldn't stop. Dark streaks ran down her legs. Your grandmother wasn't warm-hearted, but for once she didn't say one unfriendly word. She swaddled Hilda in a coat and hurried her down the street to the hospital. I jogged alongside, sobbing. 'Don't you dare die,' your grandmother kept saying, 'a strong girl like you.'"

"They saved her," I said, taking my mother's hand.

She patted my fingers reassuringly. "Hilda had a good life in the end. She married her lover and everybody pretended it never happened." My mother looked into my eyes then, and her gaze softened.

I understood then that she was the opposite of deceptive. My mother invaded my life to show she was interested in everything about me. My grandparents had maintained a cold shell, and she was determined to be different.

My mother placed our palms together. "Promise me we're done pretending. We'll tell each other the truth."

"I promise," I said, and shook her hand.

The rain was receding, leaving the leaves freshly washed.

"Fabulous. Over a potato dinner, we'll start by talking about the fellow you're rooming with. And you do know that wearing this black blouse with black trousers creates a negative mood, don't you? You're a smart and funny person; try to look like one."

I smiled. "He's my husband. And I think black suits me."

For once, my mother's criticism seemed like a clumsy declaration of love.

Christine I. Peters is a German-American university educator from near Heidelberg, who moved to Marin County, California, seventeen years ago. She spins stories from conversations she hears at surfer cafés, in checkout lines, and at her mother's ladies' teas. Christine has a husband, three school-age children, and three tortoises.

Anatomy of a Breath

Rina Faletti

E ndless strings of tiny events occur on any given day when my mother's life is suspended in the balance in the ICU, breath sustained by a machine, bowels stilled, lungs in trauma: each breath a report, each eye flutter a remark. I lean in vigilance toward her bedside for twenty-one days, the outside survival limit for a patient of her age on a respirator.

A long time before, at the beginning, when I heard the pulmonologist say she might be on the respirator for several weeks, I froze. I had already been riveted to her bedside for four eternal days by then. I could not imagine her in the ICU for weeks.

Now, I shake my head and wonder: *What is an hour? What is a day? What is a week?* I learn that time means nothing. The clock nods: slip needle into catheter, write down numbers: pressures, gasses, beats, breaths. Twenty-four times a day. Phone calls, bedsheets, eleven IV bags. Her eyes, disbelieving. And waiting replaces time.

In my family, we take vibrancy for granted. I am not surprised her sense of humor rises, even while she lies in critical condition, tied together with tubes. The hospital staff adores her. They squeeze her hand and call her *Honey*. She pats their arms. She gives them the thumbs-up. She jokes with her eyes. She is conscious the entire time.

I drive from the hospital back up to my mother's hilltop house, the home I grew up in. I try to remember to eat, try to practice breathing while the whispered voice counts down these long, long days. Try to write this down. To speak with that silent voice, pen against paper, fingers along keys, that voice that vibrates with a different kind of air, creates a silent kind of sound: the internal voice that speaks what the other voice cannot say.

I work in a makeshift guest bedroom office, a space sparse and unfamiliar, a shadow of the room I once knew. Back then, twin bunk beds balanced against walls, a bright newspaper kite hung suspended, closets full of storybooks beckoned, sinister clown pictures deceived us in the dark. Now, my computer wobbles on a nightstand too short for the dining room chair. I bend to type, knees splayed, squinting past my blue-screened reflection. What if I turned off the monitor and typed invisible words on an unseen page of glass? Would my writing find her truths? Would my words catch her breath? Perhaps grief can't be caught in words, for, like light, grief is weightless, empty, a vacuum of being, the loneliest sound. It is a breath drawn on impulse, an effortless release up toward the long, open passage toward light, that unconscious rush of air meeting air. Where the vocal cords touch, just below the mouth of the airway, do oscillating waves of grief become sound? I write under my breath: *To grieve is to find the place where the two sides meet.*

Mom's dog, Emily, pads in, slumps softly to the floor at my feet into a pile of long golden fur. Writing: I moan aloud when the agonizing words strike, and she starts, head up, nose pointed into its ancient retrieval pose, scenting threat. I force my fingers to move on the keys, even when grief begs me to stop. How much time is left? How many keystrokes must I take to tell it?

⁓

Within the first few days, Mom has devised signals. She taps her fingers and feet, scratches her nails on the blanket, swims her feet. When I look up, she fixes her eyes on mine and her index finger swirls the air. I prop the clipboard on her abdomen, supporting its weight above the incision, dressed but open and unsutured, under a pale blanket. I hand her a pen. She frowns to focus morphine-glazed eyes, concentrates the point into place on the page, scratches out invented words that direct themselves briefly toward the margin but then dribble like spittle down the page. She writes "HT": I wrap ice in a cloth and lay it on her forehead, cool her face and her hands, pull the sheet off her legs, let her skin breathe.

One day she writes "ATTY." I find a notary public willing to witness a power of attorney in the ICU. Mom scrawls across the page in a ragged, unrecognizable script. I watch her eyes. She looks back and nods, the "O" of her lips circling the accordioned blue tube, the slight movement of her head pulling at the nose tube and tugging at the tangle of IV lines as she labors.

In these ragged hand motions and wide eyes, I hear a desperate voice. She coughs to clear her lungs: no sound, only a heave of air up the plastic tube that parts her vocal cords, stilling their vibrations. Hollow gurgles emit. In sudden pain, she motions for the pen, face reddening, eyes direct and round, fierce in their openness. A nurse comes in to suction her lungs. Mom's eyes flash with fear. Then she closes them, and tears stream down.

⁓

Now, weeks later, on an otherwise forgettable Wednesday, twenty-one days after the first surgery failed, I look up from the keyboard and notice the clock, puzzled that time has not stopped. It is just before three in the afternoon, the last day Mom can safely be on the respirator without crossing that forsaken line. Nausea's butterflies flutter, gnaw with an emptiness I am used to now. The only remedy for these beating wings of fear is to see her, to be near her body, alive. I ward off the flutter, close the computer, and drive back down the hill to the hospital.

Looking up from the hospital parking lot, my eyes follow the long curve of the foothills' ridge, an elevated horizon. At this time of year, mid-May now, hills are emerald, trees lush and leaves waxy, air soft and moist. It will rain this afternoon. Clouds billow in from the ocean, roll over each other in waves of grays. This is the familiar air a Northern California spring rain brings.

I breathe in and swallow the heavy air. I inhale star jasmine and sage, a mix of cultivated and wild. Trees rustle. My hair blows into my face, and I sweep the stray locks away. I say hello to an ambulance driver I recognize, and a familiar nurse greets me like we've known each other all along. The doors of the hospital whisper me in.

After a moment's pause at the desk, the charge nurse buzzes me into the ICU, and I approach Mom's room, curtains pulled back to reveal the ward's transparent bowl. There she lies, on the other side of the glass.

I enter. Her wide, open eyes catch mine, hold my gaze. They seem too round, too concentric, pupils and irises and whites arranged in a perfect bull's-eye. Something is different.

Then, sudden as breath, I notice. My hand comes to my mouth as I gasp, and my own eyes open wide, and the tears sting.

Her mouth is closed. Her lips touch: the two sides meet, skin against skin in a soft line. No plastic tube. The respirator stands in a corner, the machine dark and cold and quiet, its long blue tube slung like an old hose: useless now, unnecessary.

She motions with her finger for me to come to her side. I bend and kiss her forehead. She beckons again, looking into my eyes, crooking her finger near her face. I lower my face to hers. She draws the smallest of breaths, and in the hoarsest whisper she croaks, "And I can talk."

⌒

Later, back at the house, I break from writing this all down to put water on for tea. I breathe in as the hot liquid steeps, warm mug nestled in my hands. Behind picture windows, I look down the canyon, watch the storm move up the wide valley. The gray storm front rises in a long roll and pushes its way toward this place where I stand behind glass, looking out. Ocean winds goad the gray clouds up the canyon like breath up an airway. The pepper tree shakes its head and the rain arrives. It patters against roof and windows, pelts the pyracantha and the ivy, the bearded iris and the ice plant's anemone flowers. Drops fall harder. The rain speeds the pace of its breaths, chatters upon the skylights. The storm front passes over the house, and I imagine that it passes through me. I turn my head as it moves up the creek and traces the road to the head of the canyon. There it hangs, above the lip of the hills, breathing over the open valley like an exhalation against the cold.

It rains hard now, and the whole valley breathes with its song. I open my mouth and I breathe a vocal sigh, my song, above the hum of the free, falling rain.

Rina Faletti is a writer and teacher with an MFA in creative writing from American University and an MA and PhD in art history from the University of Texas at Austin. She writes memoir, poetry, creative nonfiction, and about California environmental history. As an art exhibition curator, she organizes exhibitions that respond to environmental crises. Her most recent exhibit, "Art Responds: The Wine Country Fires," is a one-year invitational anniversary of the 2017 Napa-Sonoma firestorms, from which she and her family were long-term evacuees.

Circles

Jessica O'Dwyer

The Guatemalan searcher I hired to find my daughter's birth mother, Ana, told us to meet in Panajachel, the town guidebooks refer to as Gringotenango. "In San Luis, where Ana lives, they don't see a lot of white people," the searcher explained, referring to me, the white adoptive mother. "Better to meet someplace else."

That first meeting happened when Olivia was seven. Most of the photos I took from the reunion are blurry because I was crying too hard to keep my camera steady. To see Olivia and Ana fall into each other's arms and hold on as if afraid to let go left me shaking.

Their black hair and brown skin, their slim bodies and elegant fingers, their quietness and ability to be still in a way I've never witnessed in anyone else; if I ever doubted the invisible bond of blood, meeting Ana convinced me of its presence. My daughter seemed to feel the same. She stared into Ana's face as if amazed. Here, finally, she saw herself reflected.

Since then, Olivia and I have visited Ana every summer, spending time in Panajachel with her and Olivia's older half-siblings, Dulce and Santiago, and Olivia's grandmother, Abuela. Like many adoptive parents, I believe reunion helps a child feel whole, filling in the blanks: *Who am I? Where did I come from? Does anyone look like me?*

Our routine is always the same. We wait at Panajachel's one gas station for the chicken bus from the mountains to arrive. Ana clambers down the steps of the bus in her woven skirt and embroidered blouse, and straight into Olivia's embrace. Dulce and Santiago climb down next, setting off another round of hugging. Finally, Abuela appears and the group opens to include her.

Later, we share a meal at a restaurant. Olivia and her siblings play cards and draw pictures while Ana and I pore over the latest photo album. The family speaks K'iche' as well as Spanish, and Olivia's and my Spanish skills are still developing. Yet somehow everyone communicates.

Ana told no one about her pregnancy. She was in her mid-thirties, a widow, and Catholic, when she gave birth to Olivia in a clinic ten hours away from her home in the town where she worked. In villages like San Luis, women who give up children for adoption are scorned and reviled. Sometimes they are forced to kneel on broken glass. Sometimes they are covered in tar. The day the searcher knocked on Ana's door with a letter from me was the day Ana's other children learned of Olivia's existence. To keep the family protected, Ana made them promise not to share the news. Still, since our first meeting, they've treated Olivia as one of their own, accepting her as their full sister.

On a Tuesday in July when Olivia was thirteen, Ana arrived in Panajachel by chicken bus at the appointed spot at the appointed time. But instead of clambering down the steps with Dulce and Abuela, she climbed out the bus's back door alone. "Today, we will meet at my house in San Luis," she told us. "Dulce's new baby is too young to travel. Abuela is too old."

Knowing Ana had kept her pregnancy a secret, I was surprised. Nervous, too. In our trips to Guatemala, we hadn't veered far from the tourist trail, and San Luis was too small to appear on a map. At the same time, I felt deeply honored by the invitation.

"What do you think?" I asked Olivia.

Half an hour later, we hopped on the next bus for the return journey.

One chicken bus, one micro-van, and one uphill hike later, we stood in the lane at the gate in front of Ana's adobe house. The roof was made of corrugated tin, and wood smoke curled from the chimney. Clothes flapped in the wind on the long clothesline, and, beyond that, rows of corn grew tall and dense and green. Chickens clucked and skittered and pecked in the dirt. A single spigot supplied the family's only running water. We walked through the yard and a yapping dog ran in circles to greet us.

"What's your dog's name?" Olivia asked, and she laughed when Ana answered, "Bob."

The house had a door but no windows, and smelled of wood smoke and corn. Two pictures hung on the wall in the kitchen. One of Pope John Paul II, fingers raised in a blessing. The other of Olivia, Ana, and Abuela, walking hand in hand.

Olivia and I sat on plastic stools at a small wooden table while Ana served a lunch of fried chicken and squash. The tortillas were handmade that morning from Ana's crop; the Coca-Cola bought special for the occasion. Abuela gave Olivia a necklace fashioned from rosary beads, and Dulce let Olivia hold her new baby. After we finished lunch, Ana jumped up and dashed outside. A minute later, a hundred firecrackers ignited, loud enough for every person in San Luis to hear. Ana's daughter Olivia had come home.

Tears sprang to my eyes as I watched four generations of Olivia's family interact. We've closed a circle and expanded it. We have more people to love. And two places to call home.

Jessica O'Dwyer is the author of *Mamalita: An Adoption Memoir* and an MFA candidate at Antioch University. Her writing has appeared in *The New York Times*, the *San Francisco Chronicle*, *Brain, Child* magazine, and elsewhere. She is the adoptive mother to two teens born in Guatemala and the daughter of a former Radio City Music Hall Rockette.

DETOURS

Deviations, Not Delays

Kaitlin Solimine

The first Calliope had the longest eyelashes we'd seen, despite lacking half her eyelids. Fernlike lashes curling from intact edges. Riveting brown eyes framed by papier-mâché lids. We held her photograph up for everyone to see—

"She's beautiful!" our friends exclaimed over deep-dish pizza in West Hartford, on our way back from Boston to Newark to Hong Kong to our home in Singapore. I was going to be a mother to an adopted daughter in just three months. It was the happiest I'd been in years. Finally, the stars aligned, motherhood in my grip.

But even then I knew the path to parenthood couldn't possibly be this simple. According to the Fibonacci sequence, one plus one doesn't exactly equal two. Each number equals the sum of everything before: *The Fibonacci sequence is generated by adding the two previous numbers—0, 1, 1, 2, 3, 5, 8, 13, 21, 34, 55, 89, 144, 233, 377, 610, 987. . . .*

"And those rosebud lips!" my sister-in-law exclaimed via phone. She had just given birth to her first son. We hadn't talked to her in a year because she fell pregnant easily (on her honeymoon), and we'd been trying to fall pregnant for four years. We loathed her for falling pregnant. We loathed everyone who fell pregnant.

*Fall*ing pregnant: as if you tripped and—whoops!—a fetus implanted in your uterus.

Fall silent. *Fall* asleep. *Fall* sick. *Fall* victim (to). The inevitability. The *slant*. Falling into the *ll*'s that pu*ll*, lu*ll* us into believing this is how we are fulfi*ll*ed.

The first Calliope was born in Kaifeng, China.

Kaifeng, in Mandarin: "an opened seal or envelope."

Kaifeng: once home to China's largest population of Jews, merchants who settled in the east, following the Silk Road's promise of riches and a respite from the Holy Wars.

"How perfect!" we said because Joe, my husband, is Jewish.

But Calliope wasn't her name yet. We knew her as Lin. A complicated character I'd never seen in my decades of Chinese study: 霖. Rain over forest. Not just any rain though: *Continuous, heavy rain*. Her name matched mine in sound and signature. Kait-LIN. We were destined to be her parents.

In France they say to fall pregnant is to *"tomber enceinte."*

Tomber, from the Frankish for *to rotate, reel, sway.* Turn too quickly and you're with child.

Tomber: "Timber!" I hear. The falling trunk, an uneasy silence, a felled tree, the corpse below.

Tomber: a tomb? All those years, buried.

The first Calliope was a ruse—we never held her; she was our daughter for only two weeks.

> *Dear CCCWA,*
> *We regretfully write this letter to inform you that based on updated information received regarding the medical needs and current condition of Lin, we will no longer be able to move forward with her adoption.*
> *Signed,*
> *Kaitlin and Joe*

In the videos the agency sent two weeks after we first received her file, Calliope's hands spun in circles like a top loosened on a table. Beyond the camera, a woman spoke but Calliope didn't turn her head.

Joe was so sad he retched over the bathroom sink. I folded into the fetal position in our sweaty Singapore bed. We sent the images of our daughter to our consulting doctor, a developmental and behavioral pediatrician. A day later, I sat in bed, read her email aloud to Joe, who stroked my hair, tears dripping off my chin in the dense Singaporean heat:

> *When we see babies in these kinds of settings, we expect developmental delays. However, there are some red flags that we see as deviations, not delays. For example, her commando-style crawling (on her arms, not using her legs) is a deviation, not a delay. Her lack of spontaneous social engagement is a deviation, as is her lack of response to verbalization.*

What happened in the span of two weeks? Lin went from Calliope back to Lin and then back to a digital file we tucked into the Gmail inbox labeled "China adoption." Not our child.

How many times had we "made love" ineffectively before we *fell* pregnant? Forty-six cycles, Joe counted. Forty-four cycles before the first Calliope showed up in my inbox. Forty-six cycles before the second Calliope scratched at my womb, dug her tiny, soft nails into my uterine lining, then my heart. Snow on the New Hampshire ground after Christmas; Singapore's heat; our home, 9,394 miles away.

When Joe and I first met, I was leaving for China the next morning. Twenty years old, we didn't think of marriage or children. Our bodies pressed against one another in the local college bar, promising an intimacy we could sense but couldn't yet claim.

From the World Health Organization: "Infertility is 'a disease of the reproductive system defined by the failure to achieve a clinical pregnancy after twelve months or more of regular unprotected sexual intercourse.'"

Our love, almost fifteen years strong, diseased . . . Doggie-style, missionary, woman-on-top, feet above head. What is the Fibonacci sequence of infertile sexual positions? Does doggie-style plus missionary equal woman-on-top, and if so, does the square root of feet above head equal doggie-style? How could this kind of sex lead to a child?

⟡

The second Calliope came a year, almost to the day, after we first saw the first Calliope's photo, our daughter bursting out of my vagina so quickly I suffered a second-degree tear, her slick body still partly in the caul. Apgar score? A perfect 10.

Our daughter's heart is a hummingbird's. During her birth, our midwife stood over me, hands in medical gloves the color of fjords, reaching toward my ballooning belly beneath the water, listening for that incessant beat.

"All I cared about was that heartbeat," Joe says, months after the second Calliope was born, eating the last pint of Haagen Dazs chocolate peanut butter ice cream in the freezer.

I ate thirteen pints of that ice cream. Eight plus five equals for-ty-five pounds gained in pregnancy. The second Calliope, we joke, is made of chocolate peanut butter ice cream.

—

Did we make the right decision?

I miss her. The daughter whose hands I never held but whose shape I traced on my phone's screen, wondering if they were "normal," wondering if their folds indicated a deeper, more challenging condition than we could handle.

Fibonacci sequences are not just mathematical but their proportions visible in earthly objects—the interior pattern of nautilus shells, the spiraling petals of sunflowers, the swoop of a hurricane's mass over the Caribbean—and even in space: every galaxy forms the same swirling space-time detritus.

Here's why: divide a Fibonacci number by its predecessor and you get the golden ratio, the divine proportion of 137.5 degrees. Unfurl a rose to its inner bud, trace the protrusion of a pinecone. All the same. Nature is an efficient, strategic beast.

—

My to-do tasks are on Post-it notes scattered across my desk:

☐ *Wet cat food*
☐ *Book tour schedule*
☐ *Swim class payment*

I am a devotee of lists. Keep them in stacks in drawers. Remind myself of the crossings-off. What was accomplished. What was forgotten. I am the daughter of a mother who never makes lists. Is never on time. Stops to make jokes with men in uniform. I have always been prompt. I never speak directly to authorities, look at my feet, away. All my life, my menstrual cycle was prompt, never questioning in its perpetuity. When an egg drops within me, my hip quivers, a pinching promise screaming, "PAY. ATTENTION." And yet: one out of forty-six.

The geneticist alone cost $1,400. Asked us for Lin's photographs. Looked for asymmetries in her face. Said there was the chance of CHARGE syndrome, a collection of health issues including heart defects, growth retardation, ear abnormalities, and those striking, cleft eyelids.

The orphanage sent detailed photos: her diaper-rashed vagina, her hands pressed into stars, close-ups of her beautiful, abnormal eyes. We couldn't see anything but our perfect daughter. The professionals could see it though, that critical angle a degree removed from divinity.

We call the second Calliope "C.C." now. My mother spells it "Cee Cee." I'm unsure whether it matters what form her name takes, or what shape she'll soon trace with tight-fisted crayons on wide, blank pages.

In the video, the first Calliope was the same age as our second Calliope now, our toddler who waves at strangers, speaks seventy-five words in Mandarin and English, crawls up my leg, begging to be breastfed ("*mu ru*, Mama, *mu ru*. . . .").

Show a person a diversity of patterns and she will always pick the one fitting within the golden ratio as the most aesthetically pleasing. In black holes, too, the golden ratio persists, that Fibonacci sequence reflected in form—always following the same ratio of distance between swirls, as in a rose petal, a dandelion's core. Yet a black hole gets hotter as it loses heat. An inverse reaction? Not quite. An irrationality: when does a black hole cool down? The answer, according to one mathematician: when its angular momentum divided by its mass equals the golden ratio.

But even this Mathematical Truth has since been disproven. Mathematics: shall we believe what we see, are told?

The earth is not flat. Gravity is not fixed, can be bent by space and time.

⁓

"If this were my own child considering this adoptive file, I'd strongly advise her against accepting," said the child development specialist. "You will spend your entire life caring for this child, never able to travel or take a day off."

If my daughter were considering this file . . . Her professional opinion usurped by the personal: *I would tell her not to do it.*

For weeks we revisited the first Calliope's photographs, examined her mouth pursed below her flat nose, the soft rise of cheek to forehead, the spacing between her eyes. What would her face tell us when it couldn't say a word?

I think she's beautiful.

How did we not see it?

What symmetries fooled us into thinking we were brave, selfless enough to care for her? That we were ready to be parents to her, to anyone?

I've learned that regret and disappointment are close cousins, but one involves recognizing what wasn't, what could've been, while the other is constrained within its own sadness. Example: to find the coolest core of a sweltering black hole, you must sit where the walls are in perfect proportion to one another.

I see the golden ratio everywhere now—the starburst leaves on the Chamaerops palms outside my San Francisco window, the hair whorls on top of my daughter's head. The golden rule, we've been taught, is divinity divided. But every number has a finite end. So we stop asking questions without answers.

When I grasp for her hand, our Calliope returns my grip, her hands like mine but her fingers her father's, and together we cross California Avenue, multiples of one another, and yet dissimilar enough to be a one and a one. And alone, we equal two.

Kaitlin Solimine's novel, *Empire of Glass*, was a finalist for the Center for Fiction's 2017 First Novel Prize. She has been a Fulbright Fellow in China, winner of the Dzanc Books/Disquiet International Literary Program award, and has published in *National Geographic*, *The Wall Street Journal*, *Guernica Magazine*, and more. Kaitlin cofounded Hippo Reads, a network connecting academic insights and scholars to the wider public, and associate-produced *Of Woman Born*, a film portraying empowered childbirth.

Unexpected Transitions

Maria Dudley

"So this is where you sleep?" my husband and I asked our daughter Emma as we drove down a dusty road dotted with yucca trees. We were in a small town near Joshua Tree National Park in Southern California.

"Yeah, I usually just go a little ways into the desert so that no one bothers me," Emma told us. "No one comes down this road, except for a few homeless people."

What was ironic is that Emma, too, is homeless. The only difference is that she has a car to sleep in.

"Once, a guy knocked on my window, so I rolled it down," Emma went on. "He just wanted to see if I was okay."

Emotions rolled through me. I'm familiar with that these days. When your twenty-year-old son reveals to you that he's transitioning from male to female, drops out of his first semester of college, and is hospitalized five different times for suicidal thoughts, things feel very raw much of the time. Ever since he was little, I have been in the role of protecting him. There is a lot of letting go right now.

When Emma told us about that homeless man, I felt grateful and not all that surprised that humanity comes in somewhat unlikely forms. What a kind, caring person he was, checking up on Emma when he was likely struggling himself.

All of this started less than two years ago, when Emma (then Ethan), who had just graduated from high school, came into the family room where my husband and I were talking about nothing in particular on a lazy Saturday afternoon. Ethan's girlfriend, Katie, stood by as he said with quiet seriousness, "Mom, Dad, I have something to tell you."

Oh no, I was thinking, *please let this not be that Katie is pregnant*. When my husband and I shared a quick glance, I knew he was thinking the same thing: *That* would be a disaster.

"I've been really scared to talk to you about this, but don't worry, it's nothing bad."

I relaxed a little.

"Do you know what gender fluid means? Well, I'm sure you haven't seen this coming, but I think that is what I am. Sometimes I feel like I'm actually a girl."

He was right. We hadn't seen it at all. In fact, Ethan had always seemed more "boy" than many other little boys, loving construction trucks, rescue heroes, and helicopters. There was never any mention of wanting to play with traditional girl toys, even though I had dolls and tea sets on hand.

My husband stood there, absorbing the information, and I turned to Google while Ethan went upstairs with Katie. He returned wearing snug jean shorts with a too-tight girl's maroon T-shirt. He had put on mascara and winged eyeliner. Ethan waited awkwardly for our reaction, wanting to show us what he had been trying on in secret for the past few months. His legs were shaved, and he explained that he had been shaving them for a while but worried that we would notice. Unbeknownst to us, this was the day that Ethan had been working up to.

We hugged him. "We love you and will support you with this journey," I said. Inside, though, I had a million different emotions. Shock, worry, and bits of confusion were all mixed together.

"I should be getting home," Katie broke in, inching toward the door. This had all been hard for her too, I realized. I said good-bye and mouthed a "thank you" as she left. Katie had apparently been supporting Ethan through this for a quite a while.

We asked a lot of questions. Was this a new feeling? No, even in early childhood Ethan had wished he'd been born a girl. Did he want to take hormones? Not yet, but someday. Did he like boys? No, he liked girls and wanted to keep dating Katie. Did he want us to use girl pronouns like she and her? Either way was okay. Had he picked out a girl name? Yes. Emma.

I asked if we could continue our conversation over dinner at a casual nearby restaurant. I went upstairs to change, and I froze in front of my closet. *Is Emma planning on changing back into boy clothes, or is she going to go out in the clothes she modeled for us?*

I was not proud of my fear and anxiousness at that moment. Of course I was supportive of my child, but wouldn't people stare at us? I mean, she definitely wasn't pulling off that look at this early stage. I had to take a deep breath and let it go before returning downstairs. There would be a lot of deep breaths and letting go in my future.

I waited in the car with my husband at the wheel, and minutes later Emma appeared, dressed again as a boy in the usual Levi's and T-shirt. I could relax again, for now.

⌒⌒⌒

Many months later, during Christmas Eve dinner, after Emma had dropped out during her first semester of college due to depression, I gave our family Christmas "crackers"—toys wrapped up in shiny foil that you yank apart, spewing confetti and little toys. We all surveyed the junk that had come out. I looked over at Emma and she had a bracelet with a heart charm on it. Instinctively, I offered to trade the puzzle from mine for the bracelet. Even though I knew that Emma was on a slow transition to become a girl, I'd just spaced out for the moment. It was hard to erase those instincts.

"It's okay, Mom," Emma said. She put the bracelet on for the rest of the night, and I forgave myself for making that silly mistake.

From then on, I was on a mission to not make more mistakes. Emma had mentioned in passing that she was thinking of getting a wig since it would take so long for her hair to grow out. Plus, she wanted to see what she would look like with long hair. As I tend to do, I put this on my own to-do list.

One afternoon, I noticed that "buy a wig with Emma" had floated to the top of my list. Excited, I went to Emma and said that I wanted to go wig shopping. She didn't seem so excited. I figured she was just feeling shy and nervous. "But we can just tell the wig store people that you are in a play if that would make you more comfortable," I reassured her. I wanted to get this show on the road. I was ready to make her into a beautiful girl. We would go shopping for clothes afterwards.

She didn't budge. "I don't want to do this right now," she told me.

But I kept pressing. Looking back now, I'm not proud of how I pushed until she agreed to at least buy a wig online. It was a terrible outcome for both of us, especially since the wig was cheap and awful when it arrived days later.

The next several months contained an avalanche of hard things for her. And for me. Emma and Katie broke up, which deepened her depression. Even though she did EMT training after dropping out of college and got a job with an ambulance company, suicidal thoughts and hospitalizations became common. Therapists, psychiatrists, and medications didn't help. She eventually had to quit her job. She also started hormone therapy to begin her transition.

By the following Christmas, we'd decided a fresh start was in order. Emma moved in with my mom about twenty minutes away. One afternoon she texted us that she was feeling pretty awful. We all sat down together in my mom's front room, over-looking the bay and the Carquinez Bridge. The calming view of the water didn't bring me peace that day. We looked at Emma, and asked what we could do for her, panic in our eyes.

"I've been up all night and have come to the conclusion that I can't be here in the Bay Area anymore. I need a drastic change." Emma sat still and her quiet voice was very matter-of-fact as she said, "If I don't leave, I'll kill myself."

She had been thinking for a long time of running off to the desert, a landscape she has loved her whole life. She wanted to return to Joshua Tree where she had enjoyed a short back-packing trip a year earlier. It didn't make any sense, we told her. Running away? She had no job, no home, no transgender clinic or therapist in the desert, and no friends or family there. We begged her to reconsider. The room got quiet. It was a moment of recognition for us—we had to let her go. We asked if we could help her settle in, but she said no, she needed to find her way out of this black hole by herself. I took a deep breath and tried to let go of all my worry and fear of her being on her own.

The next morning, Emma arrived at our house to pick up the rest of her clothes and some camping gear. We helped her load her small silver hatchback. I kept thinking of more things to give her—paper towels, cans of soup, bars of soap. How do you prepare for this? What exactly is this? It's not the kind of send-off we ever expected. Our friends were sending their kids back to college after winter break. We were watching our kid drive off into a true unknown.

After Emma had been gone for an anxious month and a half with only a few phone calls to connect us, we drove to

Joshua Tree to visit her. She showed us the places where she parked her car to sleep at night. We also saw the youth center that we were so grateful she'd found—a place to do laundry, take showers, get therapy, and seek job assistance.

A couple of days later—after we'd all stayed together in a hotel, my husband and I nourishing her with burritos and other restaurant food—we said good-bye in the parking lot. I had been dreading this moment all weekend.

"You'll be okay? You still want to stay here?" I asked Emma, trying not to cry.

"Yeah," she said in her typical monotone, not at all convincing me. We were going home, and she was returning to her deserted road. Emma was becoming an adult in her own scary way, and as we pulled onto the highway and I waved good-bye, I told myself that this was her decision, not mine.

When I gave birth to my child, I didn't know that parents don't always get to choose, and that the real courage in parenting comes from letting them find their own paths. If Emma trusted herself enough to do that, then I would have to find the will to let her walk that path in her own way, in her own time.

Maria Dudley teaches writing classes to elementary and middle school students in the Bay Area. In addition, she works at John Muir Hospital, reading, writing, and telling stories with pediatric patients. She lives in Walnut Creek, California, with her husband and high school–age son.

No Telling

Li Miao Lovett

M y mother didn't plan to tell me that she had breast cancer.
In fact, she tried not to tell me, until we spoke by phone
three weeks after she discovered the malignancy. It's the kind
of family secret kept to protect your loved one.

"I nearly missed my annual mammogram. So I did a self
exam in the shower and found the lump," Mom finally told me.
Some secrets can and do stay in the shower, but not this one.

As moms are very good doing, she didn't want me to
worry. She knew I had a lot on my plate, juggling the needs of
a four-year-old while managing a household with my husband,
who had become disabled three years earlier. So why would my
mother, in her reasoned thinking, want to add more stock to
my cauldron of worries?

As soon as I found out, of course I worried. I flew to Las
Vegas to support her during the surgery.

My mother, in her usual way, made friends with everyone she encountered at the hospital. She greeted Margaret, the
surgery ward receptionist, warmly: "My friend, how long the
surgery? My daughter, she come to help me today." Between her

227

limited English skills and my father's poor hearing, it's a wonder that they had learned as much as they had about this cancer in the weeks leading up to surgery. Mom fidgeted with the flimsy powder-blue gown, careful to be discreet with those awful flaps.

Margaret assured her that things would go smoothly, but she also had a sad tale to tell. Her sister had kept her own cancer a secret, hardly acknowledging it even to herself. "My sister just powered on," said Margaret. "Didn't tell nobody until it was too late. Then she slipped away in less than two months."

Perhaps, like us women of Chinese descent, Margaret's sister wore that cloak of secrecy so she wouldn't be a burden to others, a cloak that ended up suffocating her.

When we keep secrets out of kindness, it's also out of fear of what we don't want. My mother doesn't want to grow old; she dyes her hair way too often so that her youthful features speak louder than those ivory-colored roots. And no, she doesn't want to be a burden; for her, that word is the equivalent of the other B-word used fast and loose with women in American culture. Yet once she had revealed the cancer to me, she knew I would be her ally, and she started sharing information from her medical team frequently and openly.

Except there were more secrets waiting in the wings. I was sitting on one of my own.

At forty-three, on the same day my mom discovered her lump in the shower, I had my first mammogram. Even after a more detailed exam to investigate the dark mass they'd detected, I was still holding on to the notion that my tangerine-sized breasts couldn't possibly grow anything more, enchanting or sinister. But a few weeks later I was undergoing a biopsy, a minor procedure that nevertheless induced major anxiety. Was it a benign lump or cancer? Or somewhere in between, as the radiologist indicated from the ultrasound? I pressed him for details, trying to advocate for myself as I had been doing for my mom.

I didn't tell my mother; she'd just had surgery and was awaiting chemotherapy and radiation. I kept my secret for the same reason she'd kept hers, with an added twist: I didn't want her to worry *needlessly.* How much energy do we women expend on things that, as my husband's grandmother used to say, "you *know* will take care of themselves." In all probability the lump detected in my breast would be benign. Why create all the fuss? In two weeks I would know the nature of the dark mass whose dimensions were marked like crosshairs on the ultrasound screen.

For two weeks this bit of dark energy, along with the titanium marker detectable only to strangers in medical facilities, resided in a small universe inhabited only by my close friends, my husband, and my son. Everyone I counted on, except my mother.

"Mommy went to the doctor," I told my four-year-old, "and he stuck a long needle inside my body to help me." My son understood that needles are generally bad, but he figured the doctor must have given me a lollipop. And he understood that secrets are not meant to be leaked.

My mother grew up with six younger siblings in tropical Taiwan. Erase the image of an American-style dwelling from your mind; their apartment had no privacy, and an open sewer trench separated the lower from the upper levels. Here, secrets buzzed louder than mosquitoes in bedrooms the size of walk-in closets. You couldn't possibly keep one here. Perhaps you could hide in the bathroom, but eventually the large flying cockroaches would chase you and your secret out.

I am usually not a good keeper of my own secrets. My mother possesses the psychic ability to detect some act of commission or omission on my part, and then she manages to wring the truth out of me. This time, however, the stakes were higher.

And it was a strange coincidence that my very first mammogram took place on the same day that she stepped in the shower and allowed her fingers to guide her to that festering lump. At the time she didn't know its true nature, this wicked animal that grows in stealth, this brilliant guardian of secrets.

These details and ironies I stashed away; they reawakened my faith in a higher power as the events unfolded, hers made visible by scalpel and secret-telling, mine still under cover.

It was like the phases of the moon. From February 15, the day of discovery, to the beginning of the next month, I was in the dark about my mother's cancer. The day before my biopsy in March, she left a phone message in that familiar Chinese-mother way, repeating for the sake of repetition that I *must* take care of my health, that it was paramount with a toddler in tow and a husband whose physical capabilities were now limited. I was not surprised that once again, Mom knew without me telling her.

As a grown daughter, I had every reason for restraint in telling her about my biopsy. I did finally break the silence, after the biopsy revealed that I was basically fine. Diagnosis: fibroadenoma. A big word for a benign mass. Now I could tell her everything, although she still found room for maternal worry.

"You should get it taken out," Mom said. Her message: *Things may be fine now, but what does the future hold?*

My mother's cancer and my fibroid diagnosis were out in the open, but that wasn't the end of it; secrets beget more secrets. I do not tell her that every year since that first mammogram, I've gotten the same form letter, rather ominous in tone: "We are pleased to tell you of your results . . . But dense breasts can make it hard to detect cancer in the mammogram." Should I suggest to Mom that she should worry about my small, dense breasts? I think not.

Mom's hair has grown back thicker, and her dragon nature doesn't miss a beat. As I see her bustling about during a recent visit, eager to feed me and chattering about so many things at once, it's easy for my worries to slide back into the recesses of my mind, along with all those secrets. For now, I let them rest where they are.

Li Miao Lovett stopped being a good Chinese daughter in her twenties. Nowadays she's trying to be a good enough mom to her ten-year-old. She is the author of the novel *In the Lap of the Gods* and has contributed articles on science and environmental issues to KQED's *Future of You*, the *San Francisco Chronicle*, and other publications. Li judges the Intercultural Essay in the Soul-Making Keats Literary Competition and her work has won awards or finalist standing from *Stanford Magazine*, *Glimmer Train*, *Writer's Digest*, A Room of Her Own Foundation, and the James Jones First Novel Fellowship.

It's a Girl!

Meagan Schultz

The crocuses are just beginning to emerge from the ground in Wisconsin on the day Olivia is born. Nine pounds three ounces, twenty-one-point-five inches, with a ton of hair, lashes, and brows. That's what I've been told anyway, along with the rest of the family, in a group text from my brother-in-law.

He attaches a picture of my sister lying on the table in the operating room in California, eyes slightly glazed but smiling triumphantly at the camera in front of the curtain, while the doctors stitch her back together. My brother-in-law holds the tightly swaddled newborn near my sister's head, tilting her for the requisite post C-section photo. I can't see his mouth under the pale blue mask, but I see from the shine in his eyes and the crinkle of his nose that he is grinning.

And I sit in Milwaukee, my own eyes red and puffy. Twenty minutes before the wonderful news about my niece, I am pushing my one-year-old and three-year-old boys up the driveway in the double stroller when I get a call from my doctor. He asks if I would like to discuss the results on the phone or come in. We're returning from a walk to the lake, my longest walk since being discharged from the hospital a week ago after a messy miscarriage and a follow-up uterine surgery to remove the remains of the fetal tissue.

I don't understand why he'd want me to come into his clinic. "You can tell me on the phone," I say.

He clears his throat after a long pause. "So the lab results came back; your baby has Turner syndrome."

Has?

I am confused by his use of the present tense and even more confused when he tells me the next step is to see their perinatologist and schedule an amniocentesis for this baby.

What baby?

"Wait, do you mean I'll need to do this if we ever get pregnant again?" I say slowly, with an audible sigh. He is silent, and it angers me that I must clarify this for him. "I don't have a baby anymore," I tell him pointedly. "You did the D and C last weekend."

Remember, I want to tell him, *the bright sterile room, the white lights, the cold operating table, the shiny metal instruments on the tray next to you, the stirrups, my tears?* But I say none of that.

I hear him shuffle his papers in the background. "Meagan Schultz?" He says my name and I hear the light bulb click in his head. "Oh yes, I'm terribly sorry, so yes . . . yes, this result explains your miscarriage last week."

He's not up on his Turner syndrome. He says he hasn't seen a case like this in a long time. Again, I hear him shuffle papers, looking for some information to give me that might somehow make me feel better across the telephone line. I don't ask him what he means by "a case like this."

"This wasn't your fault," he says finally, the confidence returning to his voice after his blunder. "There is nothing you could have done to prevent this or cause this. It's just a genetic anomaly."

This makes me feel slightly better. But not really.

Turner syndrome only happens to girls, he tells me.

Something about a missing X chromosome. But I can't recall high school biology fast enough on the phone to follow his scientific explanation. I'll look it up later.

A daughter. A sister for my sons. I look up at these two boys and wonder what kind of protectors they would have been, how sweetly they would have played with her. Tears well in my eyes at the thought of a tow-headed little girl running up the driveway with them.

"Don't worry," the doctor says, jolting me from this melancholy. "You can try to get pregnant again without concern that you'll have a greater chance of this happening. It'll still be one in two to five thousand."

Fuck me. Really? That ONE has to be me?

My brows furrow as my sorrow turns to anger yet again.

William, my one-year-old, sits patiently in the stroller for this entire conversation. Silas, his older brother, drags last summer's beach toys from the garage and then attempts to put his roller skates on by himself. I hang up the phone and wrangle them inside for lunch.

"Skates off," I say to Silas at the threshold of our back door, gently lowering Will to the ground.

He clumsily step-skates his way to the door and attempts to enter with us. "NO," he shouts, "skates stay on."

"Not for lunch, sweetheart," I force myself to say with a smile. "We can skate later this afternoon, after nap."

"NO, Mama, NO," he cries and throws himself down on the porch in a fit that could quickly escalate to tantrum proportions. He's hungry; I've left it too late for lunch. Taking a deep breath, I decide to switch tactics, offering him a hug instead. He bitterly accepts, then sulks inside after shaking off the plastic skates.

Bacon is sizzling in the pan when the texts begin flying back and forth announcing the arrival of Olivia. I feel like a yo-yo. Excited for my sister. Devastated for me. Yet so relieved to have an answer, and grateful in a strange way that a decision

234

was made for us, that we didn't have to learn of this syndrome and then decide what to do. Then—*ping*—in comes a text with a picture of Miss Olivia, arms and legs splayed in the bassinet next to my sister's bed, her tiny little fists clenched. And my heart-on-a-string comes full circle once again.

My sister lies in the hospital bed in her light blue gown. Olivia is nursing on her chest, tufts of dark brown hair peeking out from the standard blue-and-pink-striped cap she's been given. My sister is smiling down at her daughter, covering her breast from the shot with her freshly manicured fingers. If she is exhausted, it doesn't show.

It's no easy task getting Silas up to his bedroom for a nap, and I find myself shouting at him along the way as he tries to jerk himself from my hold and nearly crashes into the mirror at the bottom of the steps. I don't scream often, so when I do, he doesn't know how to respond. He usually laughs. But this time he hears a fierceness in my bellow, and keeps crying. I feel terrible.

"I'm sorry I yelled at you," I tell him as I tuck the dinosaur sheets around his little body and attempt to regroup. "I'm having a hard day too."

He looks up at me and I can see the fear in his eyes begin to fade.

"Here's the deal, buddy: If you can stay in bed for a nap, you and I can share a chocolate cookie when you wake up. And then we'll *both* feel better. How does that sound?"

His half-smile peeks out from under the blankets. "Okay, Mama, I will," he says softly.

Will is still in his highchair when I return. Of course he is, I left him there.

Olivia latched like a pro, my brother-in-law texts. My sister is beaming, with my niece now resting in the crook of her elbow. I smile, relieved for her.

And then my own devastating news floods back as I stare at my sweet little one-year-old with the cleft in his chin who's licking peanut butter off a saltine cracker. I start to cry; I let

235

myself wallow a little. *Why me? I wanted a girl too.* But Will is staring at me, not sure what to make of these sobs. Not yet old enough to express his empathy or even his wonder. More cracker, he says, "ma cack-ah."

Earlier, during my morning coffee break(down), Silas had asked, "Mama, why you crying?"

"I'm just sad, buddy," I'd told him as he nuzzled next to me on the couch. "There was a baby in my belly, but now there's not."

"Did the baby break?"

"Yes, sweetie," I'd whispered, pulling him closer and kissing the top of his head. "Something happened to the baby. It was broken, and it came out."

This was before the call from my doctor. Before I understood why my little girl came out when she did. Before I got the news of Olivia, with her ten fingers, ten toes, and head full of hair.

My sweet little niece is here now and though I am grieving, I am happy for my sister and her healthy delivery. And glad the news came via texts. Relieved that I can convey my emotion with smiley faces and capital letters. They don't need to hear my puffy eyes. Not today.

I tuck Will into his crib, wipe down the high chair, and rinse the dishes. Today I am grateful for my two precious boys napping upstairs, and for the time to quietly process the day's emotional swings. Thankful for the cookie I will share with Silas, and for the arms he will wrap around me when he wakes.

"I love you, Mama," he says, stretching his arms above his head as I collect him from his nap two hours later. And I am reminded that whether we are four or five, we are a family. And, right now, that is enough.

Meagan Schultz lives in Milwaukee, Wisconsin, with her husband and three children and writes to keep herself sane. In September 2017, she finally welcomed a baby girl of her own. She has been published in *Literary Mama*, *Mamalode*, and *Brain, Child* magazine, and is a contributor to WUWM's *Lake Effect*.

The Art of Departure

Sherilee Hoffmann

My childhood was spent with those who had mastered a drawn-out ritual called The Art of Departure. My parents waved until the horizon swallowed you, whether you were stepping out for ice cream or leaving for a year. When my dad sold his cars, his sunburned figure blazed during the washing and waxing before handoff. As the new owners drove it away, he toasted the air with a bottle of Crown Royal. I was right next to him, toasting as well.

Growing up with that, I knew only of the never-ending good-bye—so one could guess I was not equipped when it came time for a fast and cheerful "ta-ta!" to my college-bound son.

That summer, I did not count the remaining weekends I had with him at home. It wasn't a number I wanted to know. Suddenly, he was handing us his house key on the morning of departure. I dutifully put it on our key rack and burst into tears, so fiercely that I was unable to clean the spots off my glasses. I gave him a hug and whispered, "This would be so much easier if you were a creep."

My grief made it hard to breathe. I was grateful for those who didn't try to diminish my sadness or replace it with sorrow

238

that far outranked mine, the ones who held back on the "at leasts." Friends who had lost a child, had one in the military, or endured medical struggles still recognized we shared the common ground of "we miss our child," and their empathy moved me.

Once I could see clearly again, I planned action. I had no idea what "moving on" looked like, but I was sure it looked healthy. The obvious first place was to attack The Pile: twenty boxes holding decades of dormant school papers camouflaged in every room, cluttering up my mind, stealing from the future. I set up a table in his old room, which became a sorting center to severely whittle things down to keepsakes. A huge laundry basket became my recycling bin. I put a smiley face on it, an apology to the papers.

The basket broke under the weight of Day One, its sharp, exposed ribs splayed outward like a flattened tumbleweed. I tore through box after box, efficiently sorting, choosing, and discarding like a machine. But my preteen daughter and her hawk eyes saw something in the recycle basket that I'd completely missed: she pounced on a sketch and said, "Mom, look! Can I have it?" Peering from the back of an essay was a businessman space alien standing in a vat of acid and drinking coffee. So, of course, I then felt compelled to mine these discards for more doodles.

Finally, it was time to dump the first pile, and yet something in the basket still called to me. Ignoring this tug out of self-preservation, I dumped the papers into our curbside bin.

I stared at the recycling bin that evening, an unfitting end to those precious memories. I wished for the truck to come by and remove it so I wouldn't be tempted to dumpster dive into my son's life. My husband followed my glance and said, "You know, there might be a story in there."

At dawn, I smelled diesel in the distance, felt the ground vibrate as trash trucks rode into town. I dragged the bin up behind the shrubs with the shame of someone grabbing a donut out of the office trash. I banged up my hips while bending over the edge to scoop out a pile, shreds of paper in my hair as I broke the surface again. I held the bundle tightly to my braless chest and retracted into my house, one foot back-handing the door shut.

And my husband was right. I found stories and secrets, and I knew what to look for in the next ten crates of papers. One morning became three as I mused over each layer. Spanish papers that made me curious enough to run "my mom is *gordo*" through Google Translate. I wondered what my ninth grade son really thought of me. Is *gordo* a bad thing?

I saw his girlfriend's name doodled with such care, written the same way he used to say it: forming each letter carefully because it was made of china and he didn't want it to break. My eye caught a test where the teacher marked the answer wrong . . . when it was correct. I resisted the urge to go back after seven years and tell her my son had been right.

Three days became five, twelve, then fifteen. I didn't consider this frivolous. These were becoming my visits with him now that 340 miles divided us. We texted back and forth about my discoveries. Every day, a pot of tea started the ritual. I went from mourning my son to mornings with my son.

I became transfixed by the secret world of the teenager and the deep thoughts I never heard. *"Music whirls about my head at lightning speed"*; *"You need to be smart enough to realize you don't know everything"*; *"Everything works out in the end; if it's not worked out, it's not the end."* I was amazed at the stress our kids carry; how do they stay focused with so many hormones and so little sleep? I texted him, *I have a new appreciation for all you managed. I don't think I could do it now.*

But Mom, that's all I had to worry about, he responded.

I saw new things in his geometry and English papers; his lines of numbers were ribbons, the calculus problems drawings of lace. And then the test with a score of five out of fifty. He had a girlfriend then.

I found the paperwork from when he overturned his car on the freeway at age sixteen. Not able to bear looking at the

ER report, I raced to the shredder and used the scraps to poison weeds in my yard.

By week three, I had found eighty-one dollars in hard cash, two gift cards, and food that had expired in 2005. There were pencil sketches of penises and testicles, drawn by him or, more likely, his friends. On one paper, he had written his name forty-two times at the top where a teacher had written, "*Name?*"

How often do we get to soak in our kid's childhood? He was uncensored in his schoolwork—as valuable as overhearing kids in the car during the drive. Random sentences let off steam about his parents, insecurity about muscles, fears about the future. Those moments marked how things were going in our family. As I read, I found myself wanting to make subtle shifts in how I parented. I began to speak to my young daughter in a kinder voice, praised her more. I continued to hug her daily.

Each afternoon I emerged, used up and squinty-eyed in the light of the present. I cried telling my husband what it was like to go back so far to relive our story. I found a new appreciation and compassion for myself in the summer activity lists and thank-you notes from teachers—I'd nailed it more often than I thought. I also felt a tender new self-respect at signs my true north had remained the same. I saw it in anti-bullying speeches, years of lesson plans for the art classes I taught, thank-you notes from parents I mentored.

The pile quietly and patiently hinted at one more secret. Submerged in the froth of it, insight came to me. His name! I saw, with new eyes, how many hundreds of times he wrote it, each time loudly proclaiming to the world who he was. The formed letters revealed his moods: playful, bold, or skateboard font, experimenting with signature. I found the moment where he locked in how he'd form his E's and F's for the rest of his life.

I knew I could release this mountain of papers if I at least held on to his name. Searching with scissors, I snipped his signatures, a kidnapper making a ransom note. Hundreds of versions, sorted into piles of "elementary" to "college," marking the changes of time. A hot flash crept up my body like a thermometer, which always happens when I connect with the perfect idea. *These little name tickets, these two decades' worth of signatures, are going to become an art piece.* A gallon of Mod Podge and a canvas were in my future, but for now I stored the scraps in a plastic container that once held marinated carnitas. I imagined placing them under my mattress like they were a stack of hundred-dollar bills.

With the names safely stashed, I finally surrendered the pile to the curbside bin. My shoulders relaxed, my teeth stopped grinding, and I felt honest-to-goodness hunger again. My son's status went from "not here" to "living *there*." I was able to bring myself into his room and lift off the discarded sock and pillow wedged near the headboard, exactly where he had slept on them. Moving things around released their hold on me. He was not his abandoned can of deodorant in the bathroom; he was my son, doing new things I needed to be ready to hear about. It was in this, my Crown Royal moment, that I realized I had mastered my own art of departure.

Sherilee Hoffmann is married with two children and left her unsatisfying corporate job because it depleted her soul. She has read her humorous essays at Listen to Your Mother and Lit Crawl in San Francisco. In addition to writing a book about setting boundaries on volunteer commitments, she also speaks frequently to groups on this topic. She is a fierce protector of women's voices and their writing time.

What Are the Odds?

Harriet Heydemann

I'm not a risk taker. I find games of chance unsettling. I don't play roulette or buy lottery tickets. I study statistics. I know the probability of winning the California Super Lotto is one in eighteen million, and the probability of winning the multistate Powerball is one in one hundred eighty-five million. I don't need to know more.

My one betting exception is charity, especially for students. I will buy raffle tickets and put my name in a hat to support any school program—new uniforms for the marching band, more computers for the library, new sweatshirts for the girls' water polo team.

So when the local high school held their big spring fund-raiser for their building renovation, I went to the event with my neighbors. My daughter, Ariela, was only in second grade then, but with luck she'd go to that school someday.

"One for five, four for twenty," a blonde cheerleader with a swishy ponytail called out as she pranced by with a roll of tickets.

I handed her a twenty, my gambling limit. I didn't bother to look at the prize. I never win.

Student waiters circulated with trays of mini quiches and bits of blue cheese on endive leaves. Parents dressed in red and white, the school's colors, poured wines donated by local restaurants and vintners. I inspected the silent auction items stationed around the room. The more interesting stuff—tickets to the San Francisco Symphony, dinner at The Ritz-Carlton in Half Moon Bay—were already overbid by the time I got there. Streamers were sagging and a few helium balloons had fallen to the floor. I milled around and found my way to one of the high bar tables scattered throughout the gym.

Friends joined me as a tray of sparkling rosé floated by. We were laughing about I-don't-know-what when someone at the table said, "That's you, Harriet," and suddenly, there I was, running up to the front of the room.

"That's me! That's my name!" I yelled, waving my winning ticket in the air. I nearly tripped jumping up the three steps to the makeshift stage.

A broad-shouldered football player in a school jersey handed me a red envelope. Inside was a glossy brochure with giant palm trees gracing the cover. Four days, all expenses paid, in a four-star resort on the beach in Cabo San Lucas. Round-trip airfare included. I could smell the saltwater and hear the waves inside that red envelope. My hands shook and my legs wobbled. The football player grabbed my elbow and guided me down the steps and back to my table.

⌐‿⌐

The deal expired in six months. Six months to plan our getaway. Gary and I hadn't been away together without Ariela for over four years. That time, a trusted teacher who had taught Ariela every day for over a year, took care of her in our home. But that teacher had moved, and there was no one else. We were afraid to leave her. She used a wheelchair, blinked for "yes," and turned her head for "no." There was a lot to learn about Ariela.

"She'll be fine," I coached myself, knowing that fine was relative, and nothing was ever really fine for her.

I made our reservations for October, the last month of the offer, the perfect time to go to Cabo. The weather would be warm but not too hot. We would avoid winter storms and families with small children. Healthy little kids made me nervous, scurrying and squealing like little mice. It was painful to see what I didn't have.

I put an ad on Craigslist for a new aide for Ariela. Katie was the only one of twenty or so respondents who passed my initial phone interview. Three questions: Do you speak English? Do you have a California driver's license? Can you lift thirty pounds? I wanted the in-person interview to go well. There was no second option.

Katie had just turned twenty-one and was finishing her degree in special education. She was a bright young woman with the enthusiasm of a camp counselor and the self-assurance of a seasoned professional. She wasn't just an experienced babysitter; she was a soon-to-be special ed teacher. She'd played volleyball in high school and projected a certain sturdiness. She was stocky, but not fat. She looked like she could withstand an earthquake or a tsunami. Six months would be plenty of time to train her.

During the first few weeks, Ariela put Katie through her usual hazing. Initially, she ignored her new aide, looking the other way every time Katie spoke to her. One day, on a neighborhood walk, Ariela rubbed her nose, her sign for using the bathroom. Katie wheeled Ariela from one store to another, looking for a wheelchair-accessible restroom. Ariela was insistent. No, she couldn't wait until they got home. Finally, Katie found one for employees only in Safeway. Once in the bathroom, Ariela started laughing. She didn't really need to go. She was only teasing.

Katie smiled when she told me about the incident. She appreciated Ariela's sense of humor, even when she was the target.

They eventually bonded when Katie aided Ariela at summer day camp. She held Ariela in the pool, assisted her at the crafts table, and pushed her around the playing field in games of tag. They shared a competitive spirit. The two of them won a lot of ribbons. Ariela's grin told me she was pleased with her new playmate.

Katie took Ariela to her therapy sessions and studied her medical protocols. We had a plan and a backup plan for all emergencies. All questions asked, answered, and documented in a notebook for her reference. Pediatrician, nearest hospital, Gary's mother in San Francisco (who was too old to do much, but was at least someone to call). Katie assured me she could handle any event, large or small.

Gary wasn't so sure. He was nervous about leaving Ariela. "Three hours in the air, when we can't be reached. That's three hours each way," he warned me a few times. He always envisioned worst-case scenarios.

"Right. And an asteroid will hit our planet in the next fifteen minutes." Hyperbole was my best weapon with him. "Nothing bad will happen," I reassured him, burying my own doubts.

I worried about my fragile daughter who couldn't tell me where it hurt and how much. More than once, I had snuck around the camp center or the school playground, hid behind a fence or a bush, and watched her. I would miss her during those four days, but I desperately needed a vacation from worry, if that were at all possible.

<hr />

By September, I was dancing as I walked, all giddy, like a little kid. I giggled when I talked about our trip and sang to myself, "I'm going to Ca-bo; I'm going to Ca-bo." The beachfront hotel in the brochure beckoned us to park our pale bodies on lounge chairs under an umbrella in the sand. I'd read a novel or two. Gary would swim in the ocean. We'd watch the tide while bare-chested waiters in white shorts and sombreros served us mojitos and fruit-flavored ices. Gary and I would take long sunset walks along the shoreline. I could already feel my toes in the wet sand. We'd sleep late every morning with the steady roar of the waves just beyond our private patio. I had never felt so lucky.

I bought a new swimsuit in an aqua blue called Calypso and a gauzy white beach cover-up and sunscreen with extra-high SPF. What else could I possibly need? I was packed a week before the trip.

The day before our flight, I raced around town, occupying myself with a few last-minute errands—refill Ariela's prescriptions, stock pantry with snacks for Katie, return library books. On my way home, my cell phone rang.

"Ariela had a seizure," Katie cried out, her voice frantic. She was gasping for air. Then she started to sob, heaving into the phone. In the past six months Katie had observed Ariela's seizures, but I had always been there. "I've never seen anything as big as this one. I can't do this," she whimpered. "I'm scared."

"Is she all right?" I'd never called 9-1-1, but there was always a first time. I held my breath.

"Yes. She's sleeping now." Katie was still sniveling.

That was all I needed to know. Ariela was safe. This crisis was over. I could go on exhaling and inhaling until the next one.

Then Katie blurted a bunch of nonsense I couldn't understand. Her mumblings reverberated inside my head. "Enough!" I wanted to yell at her. Katie was backing out. I knew we couldn't leave Ariela alone with her or with anyone else after that.

I had trusted Katie. I had spent six months coaching her, not just on Ariela's care and routines but on her own academic choices. I'd even listened to her woes about her jerk of a boyfriend.

When I got home, I went straight to Ariela. Katie wanted something from me—acknowledgment that she had managed the seizure, that she had followed protocol.

I ignored her. I couldn't bring myself to look at her. She had robbed us of our one chance to get away. She might as well have stolen my ATM card and drained my bank account. Worse. I had depended on Katie, and she had reneged on her promise. So I did the only logical thing. I vowed to hate her for the rest of my life.

We were able to turn in the plane tickets for a cash refund. We forfeited the hotel. Gary was relieved about the canceled trip and happy with the extra cash. At the time, I wasn't working. We needed the money more than the trip.

Katie soon got a job as an aide for a boy with disabilities. When that boy's mother heard that I had trained her, the mother hired her on the spot. Her son didn't have epilepsy.

~~~~

I knew the statistics. Each year forty-eight out of every one hundred thousand people in the US will develop epilepsy. Ariela had her first seizure around age three. It happened without warning, while she was eating breakfast. I gazed at her with a mixture of fear and bewilderment. I had no explanation for her odd jerking.

By the time she was seven, she was taking several anticonvulsants. None controlled all of her seizures. Most were over and forgotten in a few seconds. Others lasted longer. The exact timing, intensity, and duration of Ariela's seizures were unpredictable. You didn't know if there would only be a little rumble, your wine glasses tinkling in the cabinet, or if the roof would fall on your head. You didn't know if you could forget about it the next minute, or if it would never stop. They could happen anywhere, anytime, day or night. Anything could be a trigger. There was no cure.

About one in one thousand people with epilepsy die each year from a seizure, a risk far greater than an earthquake or a tsunami or an asteroid. And much greater than winning the lottery. I had never shared that statistic with Katie. I had put it out of my mind and tried to play the odds.

I had given Katie a task of undetermined proportions, involving unspeakable consequences. I had expected her to take a risk that I myself would never have accepted if our roles had been reversed.

As Ariela's mother, I lived on a fault line, teetering on uncertain ground. How could I have expected Katie to stand in my place? I looked at my swimsuit folded in my drawer, wondering if Gary and I would ever be able to get away.

Harriet Heydemann is a memoirist and MFA candidate in creative writing at San Francisco State University. Her work has appeared in *The Sun, Hippocampus, Brain, Child* magazine, *The Big Roundtable, A Cup of Comfort for Parents of Children with Special Needs,* and elsewhere. She has also read at Listen to Your Mother San Francisco.

She Loves the Game

Nancy Devine

L ast week I had a dream in which my elderly mother was
sitting in a huge, old-fashioned baby carriage instead of
her wheelchair. I didn't question the carriage, but was stunned
when she repeated a comment about my best friend that she
could have only read in my personal journal. What hurt most
was the fact that we'd been over similar territory back when I
was in middle school.

I'd come home early from seventh grade one day and found
her in my room, stuffing my red diary back in the bookshelf.

"What're you doing?" I'd cried out.

"Delivering your clothes, washed, and folded," she'd said,
her voice warbling. She spun and patted the clothes on my bed.

"Not in the bookshelf," I'd said flatly. I felt my face flush.
"My diary's my private business."

"Everything at home is my business," she'd snapped. She'd
fingered the simulated pearls she wore with her pink shirtwaist
dress. "You should be grateful for all my work for you."

"I *am* grateful, but my diary is private. I'll wash all my
clothes so you leave my diary alone." My head throbbed. She'd

tried to cover up her snooping, and now she was hoping to make me feel guilty. I did lots of my laundry already. I was mad, and embarrassed for her, a disturbing new feeling.

"You wouldn't have a diary, or anything, without me," she'd said, her voice shrill. She hurried into her bedroom and closed the door with a bang.

I understood my parents supported me, but my mother had crossed a big line. And she wouldn't say why she'd read my diary. I wasn't the kid who caused trouble at school—the real mischief-makers scared me. I wasn't truly devious enough to spy on.

I pulled out my diary and found it unlocked. My last entry was about laughing so hard at lunch that I knocked my books into a flowerbed. I locked it and tucked the key behind it, my stomach twisting. At dinner, I didn't eat much and excused myself early for homework. Back in my room, I wrote in my diary about what happened with Mom. Maybe I was daring her to read it. Lying in bed, I felt like I'd lost something I couldn't name. The next morning, I looked up the word "betrayed" in the dictionary and felt the sting of recognition as I read the description matching my swirling emotions.

Now, in the dream, many decades later, I desperately needed to make a request, adult daughter to mother. I sat on the chair near her carriage. I wanted to start simple and clear.

"Mom, when you come across my writing," I said, "what do you do with it?"

She gazed at her fingernails. "What comes across in your writing?" she asked.

I smiled. "That isn't exactly what I'm asking about." I could tell I had to rephrase.

I leaned down to her eye level. "When you find my writing notebook, what do you do with it?" I asked.

"I like it," she said. "Because you did it." This was the perfect answer from someone who toyed with the vagaries of having age-related memory loss. True, she had answered—just not the question I'd asked. She liked and played this game often. She was still as wily and willful as always.

"You're sweet," I said. "But in this case, I'm talking about action. If you find my journal, I want you to leave it where it is. It's writing I'm not ready to share."

"I won't share it," she said, shaking her head side to side, clearly channeling her favorite Shirley Temple films with Shirley's everlasting bouncing curls and a stubbornness that went for cute then.

I put my hand on hers. "I actually want you to leave it alone, okay, Mom? I have lots of projects that aren't finished yet."

"I do, too!" she said. "Lots."

"I'm sure you do," I said, nodding, "and you wouldn't want me to read yours, right?"

She coughed and cleared her throat. "Oh, I don't mind," she said. "When you get to my age, it's all okay." Here she had neatly directed the conversation to her age so I could tell her she didn't look her age.

Instead, I rubbed her legs, which often become cold from inactivity. "Mom," I said, "I respect your privacy, so I'd never read a letter you were still writing. I'd like you to respect mine, too."

She wriggled in the baby carriage to a sitting position. "Well, I'm not so formal."

I adjusted her blanket as I searched for the simplest approach. "Can you please not read my journals, Mom?"

She dug in her pockets, looking for a peppermint candy. "You don't have to get upset about it," she said, her tone suddenly accusatory. This quick turn was an expert move, executed with the speed and sangfroid of an Olympic skater.

"I'm not upset," I said. "I'm simply asking for privacy."

She gave me a sad look to let me know I had hurt her feelings. Speaking directly was not a style of communication she preferred. She'd rather interpret and rephrase what I'd said, even if the meaning was a bit lost. It was a formula she'd perfected so long ago, more than fifty years now. And yet I had spent years speaking with her more directly so we could converse better. Especially after Dad had passed. We'd made good progress, she and I.

"So," I said. "Do we have a deal? You respect my journal's privacy, and I'll do the same for your letters."

The immensity of what I was asking weighed visibly on her eyes and tight lips. She didn't want to discuss making a deal. What she wanted was to be able to sneak a peek at anything of mine, the way she always had.

"I suppose whatever you want is fine," she said, exhaling audibly.

I gave her a hug. She was doing a bang-up job shoveling guilt my way. If it had been soil, there'd be dirt piled right up to my chin. And at the same time, I clearly understood the complete futility of my requests for privacy.

Snapped awake by my alarm, I realized the deeper truth inside the dream. Mom had shown she was functioning mentally, no matter how frustrating she was. I had to come up with my own solution—maybe move my journals to the car. Not ideal, but at least Mom was still taking her own swings at life, still engaged, and able to turn a conversation with a handful of her favorite moves. Still game at ninety-four.

Nancy Devine's work can be found in *Revolution House* and *eleven-eleven*, and read aloud at Flash Fiction Forum in San Jose, California. She earned an MFA at California College of the Arts in San Francisco and a Certificate in the Teaching of Composition at San Francisco State University. When not writing, teaching, or tutoring, she hikes the hills and dances for escape velocity.

Tree Top Flyer

Teri Stevens

The last time I spoke with my dad was by phone, a few days before I received the middle-of-the-night call from my sister. Like most of my conversations with Dad, the topics varied like the many neon colors of his hot air balloon.

"I got a clean bill of health," he said.

"That's wonderful," I exclaimed, always eager to hear how he was faring. Dad had had bypass surgery in his sixties to replace two arteries and a valve in his heart.

"How're the troops?" he asked, referring to his eight-year-old grandson and twin seven-year-old granddaughters. I told him Alex was trying out for Little League that Saturday.

"Has he been practicing?" Dad asked.

"A little. Bill threw the ball around with him last weekend."

"That's not enough," Dad said adamantly. "You've got to work with him, have him hit the ball, know the positions, catch some grounders. Is there someone who can practice with him?"

I could hear the wheels turning in Dad's head. If it weren't a four-hour drive from his home in Nevada, he'd come coach Alex himself. That's the kind of guy he was. He once hauled his hot air balloon over and gave tethered balloon rides in the field adjacent to our house for Alex's fifth birthday, just because I had asked.

Taking Dad's advice to heart, I reached out to our neighbor's son and arranged for him to spend an hour with Alex the following afternoon.

At the Saturday tryouts, I learned all of the boys would make it onto a team—either the Minor A or Minor B team, depending on their skill level. I meant to tell Dad, but weekends are a whirl of activity with three elementary-aged children, so the day and evening passed without me ever getting to the call. Before drifting off to sleep, I reminded myself to call him the following day.

I was fast asleep when my cell phone rang at one o'clock in the morning. I ignored it, hoping it was a misdial, but reluctantly got out of bed when the house phone rang moments later. My sister Cindy was crying so aggressively I couldn't understand what she was saying.

"Dad is on the way to the hospital," I made out through her sobs.

And then I was too. Driving two hundred miles through the black, early morning, praying he would be all right, that his doctor would have answers, that he'd let us know what the next steps would be for Dad's recovery. Beating myself up for not calling merely hours before to let him know Alex was on a team. To hear his voice.

The sun peeked over the mountain behind the hospital just as I arrived, throwing rays of light over the gray January landscape. Cindy met me in the parking lot, her face pink and swollen. It was not lost on us that this early hour was our usual time to rendezvous with Dad to go hot air ballooning.

Dad had been involved in hot air ballooning since the late 1980s. First as a sponsor in the Great Reno Balloon Race, a three-day spectacle where more than one hundred hot air balloons take to the sky in waves, filling the pale blue with giant spheres of Technicolor. And then as a pilot.

Dad was cautious, which made him a good pilot. Which isn't to say he didn't have mishaps—basket crashing through the top rung of a barbed wire fence as we landed too fast in the Nevada desert, or landing, successfully, in the middle island of a busy four-lane intersection because the wind had come up and it was the only place to set down. Luckily this misadventure took place during the balloon races, so police officers were already at the scene to help with traffic control.

The last time I flew with Dad in his balloon, Tree Top Flyer, was three years ago, the twenty-ninth year he participated in the Great Reno Balloon Race. The basket held Dad, me, and my husband, Bill. We waved good-bye to our family as we ascended, sent skyward by fiery blasts of propane unleashed from the balloon's burners. Thousands of spectators dotted the field to witness nearly one hundred balloons in various stages of inflation—some ready to ascend, others lying motionless, waiting to be brought to life. We floated where the breeze took us, surveying the prisms of color the tops of the balloons make when you look down on them. How fortunate I was to experience something so spectacular with the two men I loved most.

Dad's wife, Laura, was at his bedside when Cindy and I got there. The periodic hiss of the ventilator assisting his breathing was the only sound in the room. I sat on the other side of the bed and held his rough hand. Through eyes blurred with tears, I took in his soft white curly hair, pale skin, and closed eyes. When it became too hard, my gaze would fall from his face to my hand holding his.

Living in the Nevada desert wreaked havoc on my father's hands. After leaving a desk job as a finance company manager to start a video game business in the late '70s, Dad worked nonstop. Moving stand-up and sit-down video games like Pac-Man, Centipede, and Space Invaders from arcade locations throughout Northern Nevada and California; counting quarters; repairing and cleaning games—all this took a toll on Dad's hands. In the cold, drier months, he devised a way to heal the uncomfortable, bloody cracks that would appear on his fingertips: he glued them shut with Crazy Glue. It worked.

These random thoughts raced through my mind as I sat holding his hand in the surreal hospital room setting. A hand that held mine when I was a child, when I learned to skip. That guided me across the street to the elementary school playground to swing. The hand that held mine, tucked under his arm, as he walked me down the aisle, and that I later grabbed for an impromptu skip across the reception dance floor, my two sisters and cousin joining us in the fun. Of course, it was Dad who had taught us all the art of skipping.

Roughly an hour after I arrived, Dad quietly slipped away. For a short time the ventilator continued, attempting to do the impossible—keep him alive when his heart would not.

We said our good-byes through tears, not wanting to leave but not wanting to stay. Shocked that the man who meant the world to us had suddenly and unexpectedly floated out of our grasp. I took one last look, overcome by a feeling of complete emptiness and the harsh realization that the man who had lain there was gone. His body, the shell of the person he once was. His light extinguished.

Before returning home I spent two numbing days at Dad's house planning the memorial. I realized this was the last time I would be able to do something for him. There wouldn't be a burial; Dad's wish was to be cremated. An obituary needed to be written, so I threw myself into it. It ran a few days later, accompanied by a photo taken of Dad in his balloon basket, dressed in the yellow down vest he always wore, its front adorned with balloon pins from fellow pilots and past events.

On the day of the memorial, Dad should have been piloting his balloon at an annual event. Instead, family and friends gathered to pay their respects.

No wind and clear skies greeted us the day we scattered Dad's ashes. Perfect conditions for hot air ballooning. A small group of family, including all six of Dad's grandchildren, watched, for the last time, as Tree Top Flyer inflated in the cool Nevada morning air. Bright neon-colored diamond shapes circled the center of the balloon; underneath those, wide strips of bright yellow, iridescent orange, and brilliant blue traveled down toward the basket. Large swaths of black between the diamonds set off their brilliant hues.

Dad's friend and fellow pilot made two ascensions with grieving family members. And Dad was there, too, both times—and then he wasn't. Swirling down from the heavenly sky, a heavy mist of gray at first, then sparkling in the morning sun before settling softly in the Nevada soil. His last wish.

~～⌒つ

At Alex's first Little League game, three fields positioned back to back fanned out from home plate to accommodate the play of six teams simultaneously. Boys and girls outfitted in pristine jerseys and pants were shepherded to the correct field by enthusiastic parents and grandparents. I thought about Dad, how he would have loved to be there. How he should have been there.

Alex was the first player to bat for his team. I hugged the chain-link fence, camera positioned so the metal bars wouldn't appear in the photo. My persistence paid off. The image captured Alex in full swing and the ball just as it left the tip of the bat, a line drive between the pitcher and first base, which Alex tagged moments later.

I imagined Dad was there after all, in the stands, a silent spectator—watching his grandson, and watching me too. I hoped he could he see how tightly I was holding on to my many memories, never wanting to let go.

Teri Stevens is the current president and a founding member of Write on Mamas. She is revising her middle-grade mystery through the Society of Children's Book Writers and Illustrators' Mentor Program. Teri lives in Napa, California, with her husband, eleven-year-old son, and twin ten-year-old daughters.

About Marriage

Vicki DeArmon

I mark those long marriages. Twenty years, forty, fifty, and even sixty or more. I pause internally, thinking, *how is it possible?*

I look at my husband of twenty-two years.

I see him as he is now, but I also see all the incarnations of him, when his hair still grew thick on top of his head and the flash of his cleft dimples when he smiled made my heart drop, his brown eyes swallowing my own. The deep earthy smell when I root my head into his neck and rest there, the same, decades later. I think it is similar for him, the sculptured hips and shape of my breasts in his hand, now overlaid by a sedimentation that makes them indiscernible to anyone else. We have a secret language of exchanged looks that are impenetrable outside of our club of two. We are the archaeologists of each other's past, and of each other's secrets as well. All the variations we have manifested have been witnessed by this one. As long as we have each other, we will have this in the world: a profound feeling of being seen.

I've witnessed marriages implode on this very point, the point where spouses stop seeing each other. My husband and I believe we are immune to this, lulled by the story we tell each other. We enjoy each other's company best and still dream the crazy dreams we have dreamt our entire life, especially about that four-acre parcel on the hill with the fabulous, multi-bedroom mansion that will absorb all of our family gatherings. At the open houses, my husband points out a flat outdoor space for our Native American Church ceremonies and says, "We'll put the tipi there." This room will be my office, I offer, standing in the doorjamb. The four-car garage, we agree, will store all of his motorcycles.

Sometimes, though, we think about a tiny house with only space for us two, especially when the concern for our children is so acute that winning the lottery and moving to Portugal seems the best option. Afraid, we can always boil ourselves back down to just us.

I remember, early on, our pact to never reach for the D word, to obliterate divorce from the realm of possibilities, to decisively shut all the back doors. Those were young people's vows, but they have served us in difficult times. When we lost the house, when we nearly lost our teen kids to drugs and alcohol, when the question came calling, *What do we actually have in common?* In the melody that is our life, even in these situations, we have somehow managed to still sound a single, plaintive note.

But the music did stop entirely three years ago, on a Christmas, our grown children gathered in the next room. My husband, just home from work, sat exhausted on the edge of our bed. I had spent the last of our money, over his protests, for a Christmas that still looked and felt lean. He sat there, refusing to participate. I hissed in exasperation, "We can get divorced tomorrow, but today we need to go out there and be happy." In the months that followed, we wrested our way back from the use of that word, the word we'd vowed to never use. This break in the harmony lasted for months. We lived parallel existences, not daring to interact, the elements of ourselves that offended the other tucked away. The cadence of life still perked all around us, until one day we glanced at each other and laughed again. I cannot say how this happened, only that time and our resolution to stay were part of it.

Our relative longevity in marriage, as well as our general amiability, makes everyone seek us out for marriage advice. We tell them what we know. We advocate against the old adages: Don't go to sleep mad. We say, do! When you wake, your quarrel will be dissipated and not worth taking up. They say marriage is hard, requiring work, and we will disagree again. Marriage is not the hard part—life is, and regulating the self within that life. Like it has been for us, this is the hardest for them to understand.

Most of the time, our disagreements are more like play, an opportunity to connect, the jokes sliding as easily as eggs from the skillet onto our plates. We have argued over money and who is at fault so many times that now we do it in shorthand. He brings up my entrepreneurial forays, which seem risky and ill advised to him, and I his purchase of the motorcycles, which seems excessive to me. We sense the outer boundary has been reached. We retreat. Our arguments about the children still flare on occasion because it is unclear who is the better parent and whose strategy has paid off. Our kids are still working their lives out as adults. We are happy to leave this as an unsolved mystery, so we get in a few humorous jabs and then retreat again, without resolution. If we lash out, the result of a bad day, the most that happens is an eyebrow goes up and we walk away until it's time for our show to come on television. Humor and avoidance are our best marriage tools.

Our family and our community cannot picture one of us without the other, and any gap in that unity is a betrayal to all they have witnessed for the past twenty-two years. Together we are the one solid thing, seasoned, the mother and father of all, it seems, in our Native American Church community, as well as in our immediate and extended family. This can be exhausting, all their sorrows running into our own. We are immutable, standing strong, seemingly bearing the weight of it all.

As a mother, I signed up for that. But now that my children have moved out, I have resurrected my individuality, a flag I used to fly before marriage, carrying it then as my freedom and my right. But there is the dark side of this too. There are times now when my alienation from the world is palpable. My despair blooms like a wide-mouthed lily that I hold in my shaking hand as I wait with the expectation of a vase and water—which does not come, not from my husband, my family, or my community. Most days, when that soul weariness hits me, I stay in and nurse a book. I glance at my texts but do not answer them, the serrated blade of my detachment too sharp against the love that is required. My husband copes with his own demons by stringing AA meeting after AA meeting, as if thirty meetings in thirty days were still the prescription for one with thirty years in the program. His solace is in community, and here I see we are very different. I resist community, the clarion call of individuality so loud in my ear.

These differences, small seeds at first, grow over the life of a marriage. After our children left home, I yearned to have a life more about me. I would build a business of my own. The ends would justify the means and the expenditure. I was preparing myself to be the hero, rescuing us, finally, from our financial troubles. I wasn't going to share the process with my husband— that would belong exclusively to me. I ignored the growing distance between us. And as a screen, I developed another marriage mantra that ran contrary to that in most marriage manuals: honesty was not the best policy.

An entire year lapsed before my husband addressed what was going on. We sat in our living room, the house quiet. "Tell me what you are doing," he said. But in the face of his questions, I grew righteous. I thought to myself, *He doesn't see me anymore. He doesn't even know who I am.* So I attacked. I didn't need him, nor did I appreciate anything he had done to make our lives better, and I charged him with being at fault for our financial situation. These words exploded in the room, his face crumbled, and he was stunned into silence. I saw I had wounded him, and he retreated into our bedroom. I did not follow. Removed, I did not care. My husband was a stranger to me.

Trying to make sense of it all, I understood that it was not feasible for two people to travel through life at each other's side and end up in the same place internally twenty-five years later. Isn't marriage only doable if one or both agree to give up on growth and stay put in the life they have created? How can marriage absorb the changes that two individuals go through and keep them peaceably tethered? While moving forward, we necessarily leave the other behind. The impossibility of marriage seems inevitable.

The next day, my daughter called, her anxiety crackling through the phone line. *Why did Dad write that on Facebook, Mom? Why?* I went to his Facebook page and the betrayal he felt was written there in public with my name attached to it. The D word was implicated too, the first time he had ever used it. I could offer my daughter nothing but my own bewilderment. What I had said seemed not as wrong as this public proclamation. I felt myself detach even more from him. I was struck by how easy it is to lose something that was twenty-two years strong. And yet I was just being myself, the same self I had always been. Wasn't that the person my husband had fallen in love with to begin with?

At home, he turned away from me, and I could not apologize the words away. "You hurt me more than I've ever been hurt, and I cannot get over it," he told me.

More weeks passed in silence. The biggest divide of our marriage stretched, Grand Canyon–wide, between us. I plunged into grief, the feeling of loss so insurmountable that I was hurled back to my twenty-year-old self, adrift in the world, wondering how to anchor.

⎯⎯◯

The next month, the Native American Church tipi ceremony scheduled at our house meant that everyone would come and witness this divide, and I felt a mounting trepidation. Still my husband did not speak to me, and when I spoke to him it quickly devolved to the same conclusion. He could not get over it. It was out of my hands.

On the morning of the ceremony I felt hollowed out, unable to do anything but surrender.

Evening fell and we entered the tipi for the ceremony. We sat on our blankets around the outer circle with twenty-five members of our community, the heat of the fire and the Native Church songs, with the heartbeat of the drum keeping us all upright and focused on the prayer for the sponsor of the meeting as the night unfolded.

Hours later, the ritual nearly complete, the first light came in through the top of the tipi, and I was asked to pray over the morning water. I took my place in the center, looking over the fire, my community gathered around me. How could I pray for them when my heart was locked in grief and regret? When I was so separate?

The Road Man leading the ceremony handed my husband the cedar to make a prayer before I began. He stood, his face reddened with the heat, and looked directly at me, something he had been unable to do for the past weeks. His voice carried low, shaking with the enormity of his words, and his apology found me, witnessed not privately but publically by the twenty-five people gathered there for the ceremony, people who knew and loved us.

With his words, I felt the pretense of my rightness, my separateness, caving. Our marriage was not a private endeavor that concerned no one but ourselves. Instead, in the hush, I felt it as a community trust. Through the fire that crackled and glowed between us rose what was true: We loved each other. Our commitment to each other was designed to preserve the space where love could catch hold again and again. My husband walked around the fire to hand me the tobacco so I could pray for our family and our friends, and he bent to kiss me. I touched his hand, the warmth and bulk of that hand familiar and kind.

I wept then. I issued my own apology, first to him, then to the people who sat there in the circle. The ache in my heart gave way to relief as I surrendered my separate self, that self that feels unseen, unloved, and uses that as fuel to strike out in a direction that takes me away from love. That lonely place of self-identity.

Then I rolled the smoke, and with the fire blazing in front of me, the water in the pail waiting, I called for God's help as I lit the tobacco, and I began to pray and give thanks for the bonds that hold us together, in marriage and as a community.

Vicki DeArmon can't stop herself from writing painfully revealing memoir, which saves her a great deal in therapy costs. Luckily, few of her family members are readers, so it works out nicely. She also loves to read and write fiction, preferably comic. Recent publications include *West Marin Review* and *Women in the Literary Landscape: A Centennial Publication of the Women's National Book Association.*

Rearrangements

Beth Touchette

When I report that the house we lived in for nineteen years burned down last summer, the first thing most people say is, "Thank god you are all safe." Next, they ask about pets. I explain that both our dog and parrot are fine, and that the beta fish succumbed to the fumes quickly. Then, after I show my iPhone images of our now wall-less and mostly floorless living room and master bedroom, they ask about our family photos and videos.

A gulp forms in my throat as I say, "We lost all the early stuff."

Our son, Bryce, was born in 1998, and our daughter, Chloe, came into the world in 2000. We used film up until a decade ago. The dozens of well-labeled photo albums that documented their baby years and early childhoods had been stored in a now-obliterated cupboard in the living room. The film negatives had been on the top shelf on our now-nonexistent bedroom closet. Now they're all ash. The pink and blue baby books where I recorded first smiles, first steps, and themes of early parties are also gone. Not a trace remains of the videotapes that recorded my son's crazy backwards and sideways crawling or my daughter's rambling speeches to the fairies in our backyard.

My biggest regret is that I can't remember the last time any of us sat down and looked at the lovingly curated record of our family's life. There was always something else to do.

If a clairvoyant had warned me that I would lose all my possessions, I would have told her I could not bear it. I loved my Crate and Barrel Italian Olive dinnerware, the rocking chair handmade by our brother-in law, my royal blue Crater Lake T-shirt, and the Japanese woodblock print of Yosemite Valley bathed in morning light. My pre-fire self would have been livid to lose any one of them. A couple months before the blaze, Chloe shattered my favorite terra-cotta fruit bowl when she swiped the kitchen counter with her overstuffed backpack. I seethed for days.

But on that day in July, the worst happened. And yet, since then, I feel fine most of the time.

Like everybody says, all we lost was stuff, and we have decent insurance and supportive family and friends. I've also internalized the quote from Greek philosopher Democritus that I have shared with my high school chemistry students over the last twenty years: "Nothing exists except atoms and empty space; everything else is opinion." The oily rags left out on our deck created a wall of flame that encouraged the atoms that composed our curtains, couch, and bookshelves to also join with the air, to form something new and fly into the sky. Particles were only in the form of our rocking chair, dining room table, and videotape for at most a couple of decades. They were mined or grown, processed and shaped, but now they are free again, and so am I. If I allow myself.

The photos are harder to let go of. They weren't objects; they were collected moments of our children's early lives.

Before the fire, I anticipated the summer would be hard because our eighteen-year-old son was heading off to college. Maybe I finally would have looked at our photo and video archive a couple of weeks after we settled Bryce into his new dorm room, when his absence began to sink in. Probably. But without those images, it is easier to accept that Bryce is grown. The curly-haired blond who loved Thomas the Tank Engine is currently a dark-haired, articulate teen who will probably major in English.

Recently, I saw a mother delighting in explaining the life cycle of a caterpillar to her rapt five-year-old son. I thought of how I'd lost my sidekick, and then I reminded myself that Bryce never really belonged to me. Like *The Hungry Caterpillar*, he ate and grew, especially during his teenage years, and he is now a butterfly, aloft in the world.

Our family escaped the drudgery of post-fire insurance claims in late August to walk in the Sierra Nevadas with some friends. The trail often became blocked with hikers arranging group portraits against the rugged mountain backdrop. None of us felt like taking photos. Even digital images, saved in the cloud, will eventually be misplaced or forgotten. I didn't nag our children to fit into the frame and smile for repeated shots. I didn't worry where the sun was, or maneuver so that it would seem that no one but us was admiring the beautiful vista. Instead, I watched a group of fat chickadees flit from tree to tree. I felt a cool gust of wind against my face and, two seconds later, saw part of a nearby mountain lake ripple as the same breeze passed over it. We can't hang on to a child, an object, or even a moment. We can only breathe atoms in and, a couple of seconds later, breathe those rearranged atoms out.

Beth Touchette's personal essays have appeared in the *San Francisco Chronicle* and the *Marin Independent Journal*, on KQED *Perspectives*, and elsewhere. She is a science teacher and lives north of San Francisco with her partner, Reese, two nearly grown children, a golden retriever, and an emotionally needy parrot. Last year she spent most of her spare time filling out insurance claims and rebuilding her home, but this year you might find her kayaking on still waters or hiking on Mount Tamalpais.

Acknowledgments

"You've got this!" we wrote to contributors as we asked for revisions. They graciously complied, and as the book neared completion two years from its inception, one of our contributors wrote, "I am grateful for all the energy, love, support, and kindness that surrounded this entire project." We couldn't agree more.

We are each grateful for finding our perfect teammate, and for the beauty we found in every essay of this book. We have many people to thank. First, to the Write on Mamas who contributed their work and for trusting us to help shape their stories. A special shout-out to Veronica Derrick, Sheri Hoffmann, Christina Julian, Julia Park Tracey, and Mary Allison Tierney for their creative brainpower.

We couldn't have done this without our stalwart anthology teammates, Laurel Hilton and Teri Stevens, and we thank them for their unwavering support, camaraderie, and collaboration, and for championing the marketing efforts.

For her invaluable knowledge, feedback, and insight into all things publishing and so much else, we're indebted to Vicki DeArmon of All Things Book.

Thank you to those who were friends of the book from the start: Kate Hopper for her stellar editing expertise and Grant

Faulkner who supported and inspired us with his *Pep Talks for Writers* at our fundraiser at the Culinary Institute of America at Copia in Napa. Thank you, too, to the talented Brooke Warner for assistance in getting this book to print.

We are especially appreciative of our families and our friends (you know who you are!) who supported us through their patience, time, and generosity. And, to each of our daughters—who shared their strengths and whose opinions were invaluable—you've got this, too.

—Joanne and Mary

30094953R00175

Made in the USA
San Bernardino, CA
21 March 2019